Beyond Literature

SILVER

Upper Saddle River, New Jersey
Glenview, Illinois
Needham, Massachusetts

ISBN 0-13-058369-3

1 2 3 4 5 6 7 8 9 10   05 04 03 02 01

CONTENTS

UNIT 1: COMING OF AGE

UNIT 2: MEETING CHALLENGES

UNIT 3: QUEST FOR JUSTICE

UNIT 10: THE AMERICAN FOLK TRADITION

"The Drummer Boy of Shiloh" by Ray Bradbury

Cross-Curricular Connection: Social Studies

The Battle of Shiloh was fought on April 6 and 7, 1862. Thirteen thousand Union soldiers and ten thousand Confederate soldiers died—the greatest loss of life of any battle ever fought before on United States soil. Twice the number of soldiers died at Shiloh than during the four previous battles combined. Regrettably, loss of life on this scale would became commonplace over the next three years of the Civil War.

Confederate commanders Sidney Johnston and Pierre Beauregard planned the battle as a surprise attack on the Union forces who were camped near a meeting place called Shiloh church, in the southwest corner of Tennessee. Tennessee had recently sided with the Union. The Confederates hoped to force the Yankees out and to regain the state for the South.

Reaching Shiloh was more difficult than the Confederate leaders had expected. Some units took wrong turns and got lost, while wagons and artillery were slowed down by heavy rains. What's more, the Confederate soldiers had been firing their guns to see if the rain-dampened powder still worked. Beauregard worried that the noise had destroyed all chance of a surprise attack. Johnston insisted that Union soldiers had been doing the same thing and that the Union officers suspected nothing. The Confederate soldiers prepared for battle.

At daylight on April 6, thousands of Confederates burst from the woods, firing on the startled, sleepy Union forces. Scrambling into formation, the Union soldiers quickly returned fired. War raged. The next twelve hours tested the skills of commanders on both sides. Union commander William Tecumseh Sherman rode up and down his line shouting encouragement and inspiring his troops. Although he was wounded twice and had three horses shot out from under him, Sherman drove his men on. Confederate commander Johnston was shot in an artery in his leg on the first day of the battle. He bled to death almost before he realized he'd been wounded. Beauregard then took command of the Confederate soldiers.

Thousands of soldiers ran from the battle scene. The commanders on both sides continually reorganized their troops to make up for the deserters and the mounting casualties. A lightning storm lit up the battlefield the night of April 6. Soldiers got little sleep. On the morning of April 7, the Union army turned the tables on the Confederates, surprising them before breakfast with an attack. By afternoon, Beauregard and his bone-weary troops were forced to retreat. The Union soldiers watched them go, too exhausted to pursue them. The Battle of Shiloh did not prove which was the stronger army—that would take three more years. What Shiloh proved was that the South would not give up easily.

DIRECTIONS: Use the background information on the Battle of Shiloh to answer these questions.

1. Was the drummer boy in the story on the Union side or the Confederacy side? Explain how you know.

   ____

   ____

2. Who was the general who talked to the drummer boy the night before the battle? Explain how you know.

   ____

   ____

3. What was the significance of the Battle of Shiloh? How is the battle remembered in history?

   ____

   ____

"Charles" by Shirley Jackson

Career Connection: School Counselor

Children grow at different rates but certain behavior and language development are common to most children. School counselors are guided by research in child development to determine if a troubled student is behaving typically for his or her age or if the student needs some special help.

Suppose you are a counselor in Laurie's school. You have been asked by his teacher and his parents to assess his recent behavior in the classroom and at home. Your job is to decide if Laurie is acting like a typical, imaginative five-year-old, or if he is acting immaturely and needs some extra help. The following chart outlines some typical social behaviors and language development for a three-year-old, four-year-old, and five-year-old.

Three-Year-Old	Four-Year-Old	Five-Year-Old
• Constantly asks why • Shares toys sometimes • Can be reasoned with • Listens to general conversation • Understands the difference between statements, commands, and questions	• Asks complex questions • Enjoys playing with others and can share easily • Understands right and wrong • Speaks in complete sentences • Tells long stories, confusing fact and fantasy	• Asks the meaning of abstract words • Enjoys imaginative and dramatic play • Understands the need for rules and fairness • Speaks fluently and with correct grammar • Enjoys rhymes and telling stories

A. DIRECTIONS: For each of Laurie's behaviors below, use the chart to determine if his action is typical or immature for a five-year-old. Write your assessment and explain your answer on the line provided. The first one is done for you.

1. Laurie hit the teacher because she tried to make him color with red crayons when he wanted to use green. Typical five-year-old behavior or immature behavior?

   Immature. Laurie's behavior is immature even for three- and four-year-olds who can be reasoned

   with and understand right and wrong. At the age of five, Laurie should undertand the need for rules

   and fair play.

2. Laurie uses incorrect grammar, such as "I didn't learn nothing." Typical five-year-old behavior or immature behavior?

   ____

3. Laurie talks in rhymes such as "Hi, Pop, y'old dust mop" and "Look at my thumb. Gee you're dumb." Typical five-year-old behavior or immature behavior?

   ____

4. Laurie made up an imaginary classmate rather than admit to his parents that he was misbehaving in school. Typical five-year-old behavior or immature behavior?

   ____

B. DIRECTIONS: Based on your assessments of Laurie's behavior, do you think he needs some special help? Why or why not? Write your answer on a separate sheet of paper.

Name ____ Date ________________

from *I Know Why the Caged Bird Sings* by Maya Angelou

Community Connection: Learning from Elders

Mrs. Bertha Flowers could have become a mentor to Marguerite. A mentor is someone who guides or counsels another person (usually a younger person) and takes a personal interest in the person's development. The person under the guidance of a mentor is called a protégé.

A. Directions: Think about the qualities Mrs. Flowers possessed that would have made her a good mentor. Then think of someone you know who would be an effective mentor. What qualities does a person need to be a mentor? How would these qualities help a protégé? Complete the chart. The first one is done for you.

	Qualities or Skills	**How Qualities or Skills Help the Protégé**
Mrs. Bertha Flowers	1. Spoke clearly and distinctly	1. Provides example of how to speak properly and make oneself understood
	2.	2.
	3.	3.
	4.	4.
	5.	5.
My Ideal Mentor	1.	1.
	2.	2.
	3.	3.
	4.	4.
	5.	5.

B. Directions: Suppose you decided to become a mentor to a younger person. What qualities or skills would you try to encourage in your protégé? Write a paragraph in which you describe one lesson you would teach your protégé.

____

____

____

____

____

____

____

"The Road Not Taken" by Robert Frost
"All But Blind" by Walter de la Mare
"The Choice" by Dorothy Parker

Workplace Skills: Decision Making

The narrators in "The Road Not Taken" and "The Choice" made decisions that had profound effects on the rest of their lives. Of course, not all decisions are that important. It really doesn't matter, for example, whether you choose to wear a red jacket or a green sweater on any given day. Other decisions, however, are more important, such as whether you should study French or Spanish, take an after-school job or join a club, or become a baseball player or join the swim team.

Whenever you have to make a decision, it always helps to write a list of pros and cons for each choice. Then it is easier to see which is the better decision. You can use this technique for on-the-job situations as well as for personal situations.

DIRECTIONS: Think about an important decision in your life. Fill in the chart, listing the pros and cons of two choices you are considering. Then explain why you will make one choice over the other.

The Choices: ____			
Choice #1: _________________________________		**Choice #2:** _________________________________	
Pros	**Cons**	**Pros**	**Cons**

My decision: ____

Reasons for this decision: ____

____

____

from **"E-Mail from Bill Gates"** by John Seabrook

Study Skills: Using the Internet

The Internet is swiftly becoming a vital resource tool. It provides access to information in a quick and efficient manner through web sites, search engines, chat rooms, and e-mail. The most popular part of the Internet is the World Wide Web, where you can find information by typing in the address of a web site or by using the mouse to click on links that connect you automatically.

If you don't know where to find information on a topic, you can use a search engine and web sites that allow you to enter keywords relating to the topic you are looking for. With the keywords, the search engine will find the web sites you are seeking.

The secret to keyword searches is to make them broad enough to bring up enough web sites to cover the topic but narrow enough to keep the results to a manageable number. For example, when searching for information on the first moon landing, using the keyword MOON brings up too many web sites—from poetry with the word moon to pictures of the moon. The keywords MOON LANDING SPACE produce more specific information. To narrow the topic further, add NASA (the government agency that handles all space flight in the United States) or APOLLO (the names of the rockets that went to the moon).

A. DIRECTIONS: For each of the following questions, write two or three keywords that you would use to find information on a search engine. For example, to find the size of the human brain, three good keywords would be BRAIN, SIZE and HUMAN.

1. What is the best way to care for your iguana?

   ____

2. What is the weather in Portland, Oregon?

   ____

3. What is on television tonight?

   ____

4. What is the correct symbol for the chemical element gold?

   ____

5. How many people live in New York City?

   ____

6. Which is Herman Melville's most famous novel?

   ____

7. Which NBA team is in first place?

   ____

8. What are the best ways to keep your teeth healthy?

   ____

B. DIRECTIONS: Choose one of the topics in Part A. Write a paragraph on the topic or the "routes" to the topic.

____

____

Name ____ Date ________________

"The Old Grandfather and His Little Grandson" by Leo Tolstoy
"Grandma Ling" by Amy Ling
"Old Man" by Ricardo Sánchez

Cultural Connection: Attitudes Toward Old Age

Our cultural attitudes toward old age are shaped by our experiences and by the way in which the elderly are represented in books and magazines, on television, and in other media. These attitudes have changed in the last fifty years as the number of people 65 years and older has increased.

Today, under federal law, workers in most jobs can no longer be forced to retire when they reach the age of 65. Retirees remain more physically active than they did fifty years ago, and many people today enjoy good health well into their seventies and eighties.

A. DIRECTIONS: Using library or sources you might have at home, find out how old age is represented in magazine advertisements. Make copies of two advertisements that feature elderly people. Then answer the questions below.

1. Advertisement #1

   What product or service is being sold?____

   What are the elderly people doing? ____

   ____

2. Advertisement #2

   What product or service is being sold? ____

   What are the elderly people doing? ____

   ____

3. From these two advertisements what conclusions can you draw about old age?

   ____

   ____

   ____

B. DIRECTIONS: Many people continue to add to their life's work in their seventies, eighties, and even nineties. Review the list of people below. Choose the one who interests you the most. Using an encyclopedia or almanac, find out what he or she accomplished late in life. Write a brief biography of the person on the lines provided.

Poet Robert Frost (1874–1963)
Astronaut John Glenn (1921–   )
Painter Pablo Picasso (1881–1973)
Artist Georgia O'Keefe (1887–1986)
Abolitionist Sojourner Truth (1797?–1883)

____

____

____

____

"Poets to Come" by Walt Whitman
"Winter Moon" by Langston Hughes
"Ring Out, Wild Bells" by Alfred, Lord Tennyson

Cross-Curricular Connection: Science

In "Winter Moon," the poet describes a crescent moon. This is just one of the many phases, or shapes, of the moon as it revolves around the Earth. Of course, the shape of the moon does not change throughout the month. What changes is its appearance, or the way we see it from Earth. These apparent changes are caused by reflected sunlight. The moon goes through all its phases every 29.5 days.

Except during a lunar eclipse, half the moon is always lighted by the sun. However, that entire half cannot always be seen from the Earth. During the **new moon**, the moon is between the sun and the Earth. In this position, the lighted side of the moon is facing away from the Earth. The side facing the Earth is dark. During a **full moon**, the Earth is between the moon and the sun. The entire side facing the Earth is lighted.

Between these two extremes, varying amounts of the moon's lighted surface can be seen. When the moon appears to become larger each night, it is called a **waxing moon**. When it appears to become smaller each night, it is called a **waning moon**.

Halfway between the new moon and the full moon is the **first quarter** phase. Halfway between the full moon and the new moon is the **last quarter** phase.

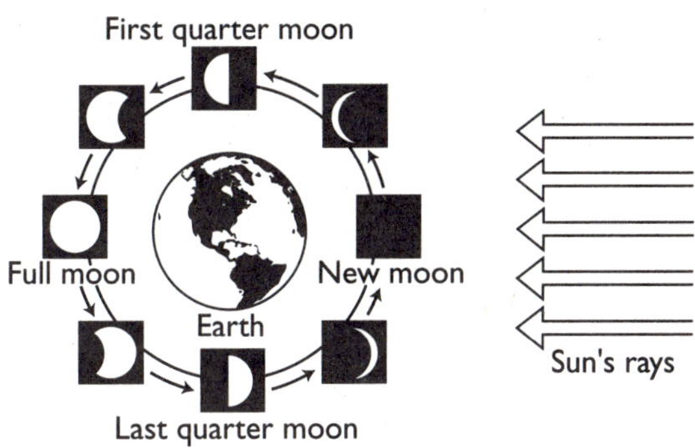

A: Directions: Refer to the text and diagram above. Match each phase of the moon in the left column with its definition in the right column. Write the letter of the definition on the line next to the phase of the moon it defines.

_______ 1. waxing moon   a. moon between the sun and the Earth

_______ 2. waning moon   b. lighted area becomes larger

_______ 3. new moon   c. Earth between the moon and the sun

_______ 4. full moon   d. lighted area becomes smaller

B. Directions: Look up the words *wax* and *wane* in a dictionary. Then use *wane* in a sentence unrelated to the moon.

____

____

"Cub Pilot on the Mississippi" by Mark Twain

Workplace Skills: Conflict Resolution

Mark Twain suffered greatly during his apprenticeship under Mr. Brown. After putting up with months of verbal abuse, Twain was so full of anger that he ended up punching Brown over and over.

Conflict at school or work cannot always be avoided. Violence, however, is never the answer. Of all the skills you will learn before entering the working world, problem solving and conflict resolution are among the most essential. Being able to recognize and solve problems early on will help you work well with others and be more effective at your job. If you feel you are treated unfairly, you should immediately discuss your feelings, respectfully, with the person involved. If the person is unable or unwilling to listen, ask advice from someone else in charge. Finally, back off or leave a bad situation before it leads to violence.

DIRECTIONS: Imagine that Twain and Brown have the chance to resolve their conflict before any violence takes place. Using your imagination and details from the story, fill in the chart to show how they could use basic problem-solving steps effectively. The first two steps have been provided for you.

Steps to Problem Solving	Specific Steps by Twain and Brown
Recognize that a problem exists (identify a difference between what is and what could or should be).	Brown continually picks on Twain. Twain says nothing to Brown about how the criticism makes him feel.
Identify possible reasons for the problem.	Brown is a bully. Twain does not know how to defend himself against the verbal attacks.
Create a plan to solve the problem.	1.
Evaluate how well the plan is working.	2.
After review, revise the plan, if necessary.	3.

"The Secret" by Arthur C. Clarke

Workplace Skills: Acting Responsibly

While on the job, science reporter Henry Cooper learns of a discovery that everyone wants to keep secret. He must decide whether he will go along with the rest of the staff and withhold information from the public or make the secret known.

Sometimes employees learn of a secret that their employer is deliberately keeping quiet. Perhaps a company is dumping waste where it shouldn't or selling a product that has been tested and proven dangerous. Employees who go public with this sort of information are called *whistle-blowers* because they let people know about certain situations that could be dangerous to the public.

Making the decision to blow the whistle is not an easy one. In telling the secret, the employees may lose their jobs or cause others to lose their jobs. They may be shunned by coworkers who feel guilty for not coming forward or who believe that whistle-blowers are snitches. They may also find it difficult to get other jobs because employers may consider them troublemakers.

Most whistle-blowers are committed to the idea of taking responsibility, believing that it is wrong to say nothing and allow an injustice to continue.

DIRECTIONS: Write your answers to the following questions on the lines provided.

1. What might happen if Cooper reveals the secret to the public?

2. What are the possible consequences if Cooper decides to keep the secret?

3. What would you do if you were Cooper? Explain why.

"Harriet Tubman: Guide to Freedom" by Ann Petry

Humanities Connection: Personal Courage

Harriet Tubman could have stayed in Canada or New Jersey, living her life as a free woman. She chose, instead, to undertake a dangerous journey time and again to lead others to freedom. Thomas Garrett and the German farmers could have turned the fugitives away but they risked their own safety to provide food, shoes, and shelter. These are heroic acts of courage in life-threatening situations.

Personal courage can take many forms. Sometimes being courageous means standing up for what you believe or doing something that is difficult but not dangerous.

A. DIRECTIONS: Fill in the following chart by describing why these ordinary actions take courage. The first one is done for you.

Action	Why the Action Takes Courage
1. Join a club composed of kids you don't know	1. Must overcome the fear of not being liked or accepted
2. Refuse to join in the teasing of a classmate	2.
3. Try out for a part in the school play	3.
4. Tell a classmate that he cannot copy your homework because it is cheating	4.

B. DIRECTIONS: On the lines provided, write about a courageous person. It may be someone you know or a public figure from the past or the present. Explain why you consider that person courageous.

____

____

____

____

____

____

____

____

____

____

    © Prentice-Hall, Inc.

"Columbus" by Joaquin Miller
"Western Wagons" by Stephen Vincent Benét
"The Other Pioneers" by Roberto Félix Salazar

Media Connection: Documentary Film

"Columbus," "The Other Pioneers," and "Western Wagons" celebrate those who left their homes and set out for new lands. The three poems vividly tell us about explorers and settlers from the perspective of the authors rather than from the perspective of the pioneers themselves.

A documentary film, on the other hand, provides a factual view of a subject. With first-hand accounts from those who were there and pictures of the event as it actually happened, we can experience the subject for ourselves.

DIRECTIONS: Write your answers to the following questions on the lines provided.

1. What do documentary films provide that poems, textbooks, or other written accounts do not?

   ____

   ____

   ____

2. What advantages do encyclopedias and textbooks have over documentary films?

   ____

   ____

   ____

3. If documentary films had existed in the days of Columbus, the Western expansion, and the Mexicans' settlement of Texas, what would you have liked the following people to tell you?

   a. Columbus ____

   ____

   b. A teenage pioneer girl ____

   ____

   c. A Native American chief ____

   ____

   d. A Mexican father ____

   ____

4. Do you think documentaries would have influenced more or fewer people to become pioneers? Explain why.

   ____

   ____

   ____

   ____

Unit 2: Meeting Challenges

"Up The Slide" by Jack London

Cross-Curricular Connection: Physical Education

Clay Dilham climbed the face of the cliff to save his life. Today, people climb rocks for sport. Different types of climbing appeal to different people.

Bouldering is rock climbing just a few feet or even a few inches above the ground. Boulderers use no ropes or equipment other than rubber-soled climbing shoes and some gymnastic chalk to keep the hands dry. Finding footholds and handholds close to the ground provides some climbers with practice for higher climbs and others with enjoyment in and of itself.

Climbing has a language all its own. Climbing the face of a cliff with the aid of a rope anchored at the top is *top roping*. Climbing without rope or gear is *free soloing*. If there aren't enough handholds and footholds in the rock, climbers may attach devices to help them in their ascent; this is called *aid-climbing*.

When a person helps a climber by holding the rope and taking in the slack, that person is called a *belayer*. In this situation, before beginning a climb, the climber calls out, "On belay?" The belayer responds, "Belay on." The climber then replies "Climbing" and is answered with the command of "Climb." During the ascent, if a climber pauses to study the next move, he or she will often shout "Climbing" before moving again. A shout of "Slack" means the climber needs more rope to continue on. A shout of "Rope" means the belayer needs to take in rope so the climber doesn't get tangled in the excess. "Watch me" means the climber is fearful of a fall. "Rock" is yelled immediately if a rock loosens and falls or if anything is dropped from above.

In addition to overall fitness, climbers need strong legs and a flexible body. Strong forearms, wrists, hands, and fingers are also important. Climbing safely often depends more on intelligence than on equipment or techniques. Safe climbers study the route to be climbed, train their bodies and their minds to react quickly, and take as much care with an "easy" climb as a hard one.

DIRECTIONS: Write your answers to the following questions on the lines provided.

1. What might make an easy climb more dangerous than a difficult one?

   ____

2. How would the following exercises/sports benefit a climber?

   a. Bicycling ____

   b. Gymnastics ____

   c. Chin-ups ____

3. What climbing terms would be used in the following situations?

   a. A climber kicks a rock loose while struggling with the extra rope around her feet.

   ____

   b. After a rest, the climber decides to continue. He then finds that he is held in place by

   the rope. ____

   c. A climber feels her arms and legs tiring as she approaches a difficult part of the climb.

   ____

"Thank You, M'am" by Langston Hughes

Cross-Curricular Connection: Math

Mrs. Luella Bates Washington Jones gave Roger $10 to buy a pair of blue suede shoes. That price reflects the buying power of the dollar back when this story was first published in 1958. Today, many people pay more than $60 for a pair of shoes or sneakers. The increase in the prices of basic goods and services is called *inflation*. In general, as inflation increases, the number of goods and services you can buy with the dollar decreases.

DIRECTIONS: Following are some items and their prices in 1960 and 1990. Calculate the price increase and then the percent of inflation for the thirty-year period. Write your answers on the lines provided. The first one is done for you. The math formulas are shown in the example.

1.

Item	1960 price	1990 price	Price increase	Percent Inflation Over 30 Years
gallon of milk	$1.04	$2.78	$1.74	167 %

Price increase = 1990 price - 1960 price

Price increase = $2.78 - $1.04

Price increase = $1.74

$$\% = \frac{\text{Price increase}}{\text{1960 price}} \times 100$$

$$\% = \frac{\$1.74}{\$1.04} \times 100$$

$$\% = 1.67 \times 100$$
$$\% = 167$$

2.

Item	1960 cost	1990 cost	Price increase	Percent Inflation Over 30 Years
loaf of bread	$.20	$.70	$__________	__________%

3.

Item	1960 cost	1990 cost	Price increase	Percent Inflation Over 30 Years
gallon of gas	$.26	$1.34	$__________	__________%

4.

Item	1960 cost	1990 cost	Price increase	Percent Inflation Over 30 Years
automobile	$2,610	$16,012	$__________	__________%

5.

Item	1960 cost	1990 cost	Price increase	Percent Inflation Over 30 Years
house	$12,675	$123,000	$__________	__________%

  Beyond Literature **13**

"Flowers for Algernon" by Daniel Keyes

Cross-Curricular Connection: Science

Modern intelligence tests are based largely on the work of Alfred Binet and Theodore Simon who created a test in 1905 called the Binet-Simon Intelligence Scale. They worked with public school children and mentally challenged children at a local hospital, trying to establish criteria for average physical and mental abilities.

They created a test to assign children to appropriate class groups and to predict their abilities in the classroom. The test was composed of questions and activities ranging from easy to difficult. A child was first asked questions designed for someone his or her age or younger. The tester asked increasingly difficult questions until the child could no longer answer them; that level was considered the child's mental age.

The term Intelligence Quotient (IQ) is used to describe the results of intelligence testing. The average IQ score is 100. Mentally challenged people like Charlie usually score below 70. Over the years, people have criticized IQ tests for different reasons. Some people doubt that the tests are meaningful or challenging to all people because of cultural differences. Others argue that some people are intelligent in some areas but less so in others and tests cannot possibly measure all the different qualities of intelligence. Today, psychologists favor tests that measure special abilities and personality.

DIRECTIONS: Write your answers to the following questions on the lines provided.

1. Do you think we should pursue artificial intelligence as shown in the Algernon and Charlie experiment? Why or why not?

   ____

   ____

2. Was Charlie happier when he became smarter? Explain your answer.

   ____

   ____

3. Why might IQ tests be helpful?

   ____

   ____

4. Why might IQ tests be harmful?

   ____

   ____

5. Why might identical twins have very different IQs?

   ____

   ____

   ____

   ____

   ____

   ____

"Brown _vs._ Board of Education" by Walter Dean Myers

Study Skills: Using a Graphic Organizer

The United States Supreme Court is the highest court in the nation. Its basic duty is to determine whether federal, state, and local government are acting according to the Constitution of the United States. About 5,000 cases a year are submitted for consideration before the Court, but fewer than 200 cases are actually heard by the nine Supreme Court justices. The cases that must be heard by the Court are those in which one state brings legal action against another state, or those in which a state appeals a Federal Court decision declaring a state law unconstitutional.

Most cases, however, reach the Court by a method called **certiorari.** This written request, which means "we wish to be informed," is prepared and sent to the Court by the opposing attorneys. All such requests are read by the justices' law clerks, who then write summaries of the cases for the justices. The justices meet together each week and decide which cases merit review. If four or more of the nine justices decide a case is worthy of review, it will come before the Court.

Once a case has been chosen, the opposing lawyers are notified. The lawyers present their arguments in written form, called **briefs.** Other interested parties may also submit briefs in the case. The justices read the briefs privately. Then the lawyers argue the case in court. During the Court session the justices ask the lawyers questions.

Once the oral arguments are heard, the justices retire to discuss the case and form their opinions. One justice is chosen to write the Court's opinion, representing the view of the majority. A dissenting justice may write a minority opinion to express his or her opposing opinion.

DIRECTIONS: Complete this flow chart to organize the steps in the United States Supreme Court process. The first and last entries are done for you.

Step 1

Certiorari

Step 5

Step 2

Step 6

Step 3

Step 7

Step 4

Step 8

Majority opinion

"**A Retrieved Reformation**" by O. Henry

Cross-Curricular Connection: Science

When Jimmy Valentine was busy cracking bank safes, he didn't have to worry about modern-day police investigative techniques. There was no Federal Bureau of Investigation, no scientific crime laboratories to help discover evidence, and no organized method of fingerprinting.

William Herschel, a British official in India in the 1870s, was one of the first to understand the importance of fingerprints. He collected prints as a hobby and ended up using prints as a way of identifying people. The small ridges in our skin on the tips of our fingers form patterns. These ridges help us grasp and hold on to things. When we touch something, oils from our skin leave a print of this pattern on the surface we touch. This pattern is our fingerprint. Herschel noticed that each fingerprint looked different, that each person created a unique pattern when leaving a fingerprint.

Eventually inspectors and detectives in police organizations came to understand the importance of this unique pattern. In 1892, Argentina became the first country in the world to use fingerprinting as standard police procedure. Soon police forces in Europe and North America began collecting these signatures left at crime scenes. Today the FBI fingerprint file in Washington, D.C. contains millions of prints. All the information is computerized and shared with state and local police agencies across the country. To help solve crimes, there are scientific laboratories, called forensic labs, in all modern police agencies. They use well-trained scientists to apply the current knowledge of forensic science to examine not only fingerprints but footprints, hairs, fibers, blood, and any other evidence left at crime scenes. There is even genetic fingerprinting in which the DNA (deoxyribonucleic) molecule of a person is extracted from skin tissue, bone, blood, or even a single strand of hair. For each person there is a unique genetic pattern which can be used just like regular fingerprints to identify the person.

A. DIRECTIONS: Compare the task of detective Ben Price with the work of today's modern detectives by answering these questions.

1. When Ben Price visited the scenes in Richmond, Logansport, and Jefferson City, what modern forensic science knowledge could have been useful to him?

   ____

   ____

   ____

2. Do you think Jimmy Valentine wore gloves when he cracked safes? Why or why not?

   ____

   ____

3. What modern communication techniques would have been helpful to Ben Price? Explain why.

   ____

   ____

B. DIRECTIONS: Answer this question about Jimmy Valentine if he lived today.

Would Jimmy be a successful safe cracker today? Give reasons for your answer.

   ____

   ____

"Emancipation" from *Lincoln: A Photobiography* by Russell Freedman
"O Captain! My Captain!" by Walt Whitman

Workplace Skills: Decision Making

The Emancipation Proclamation, the decree signed on January 1, 1863, freeing all the slaves in the rebel states, was the result of a long decision-making process. Lincoln went through a series of steps in making his important decision.

- He had a reason for, or purpose, in making his decision.
- He had objectives he wanted to achieve.
- He considered alternatives to making the decision.
- He weighed the consequences of the alternatives against the consequences of his decision.

A. DIRECTIONS: Analyze Lincoln's decision to sign the Emancipation Proclamation. Write your answers to the following questions.

1. What were Lincoln's reasons, or his purpose, for making this decision?

____

____

2. What objectives did Lincoln consider?

____

____

3. What other alternatives did Lincoln have?

____

____

4. What could have gone wrong with these alternatives?

____

____

B. DIRECTIONS: Analyze a decision of your own on the lines below.

1. Reason for, or purpose of, decision _______________________________________

____

2. Objectives ____

____

3. Alternatives ____

____

4. Consequences of alternatives ____

____

5. Final course of action ____

____

"Gentleman of Rio en Medio" by Juan A. A. Sedillo
"Saving the Wetlands" by Barbara A. Lewis

Cross-Curricular Connection: Math

Imagine that you are the surveyor in the story "Gentleman of Rio en Medio." Here is a map showing the land Don Anselmo thinks he owns. You discover that he owns a piece of land of equal size and shape across the river.

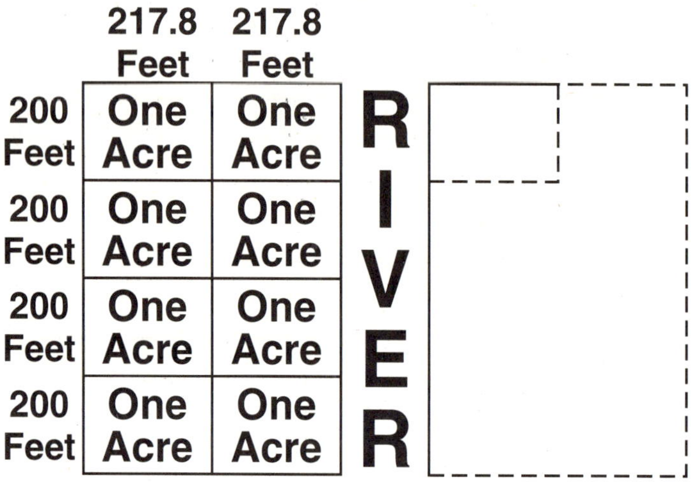

	217.8 Feet	217.8 Feet			
200 Feet	One Acre	One Acre	**R**		
200 Feet	One Acre	One Acre	**I**		
200 Feet	One Acre	One Acre	**V**		
200 Feet	One Acre	One Acre	**E**		
			R		

DIRECTIONS: Complete the diagram showing the land Don Anselmo owns across the river. Label the measurements of the new piece of land in feet, based on the measurements of the original piece of land. Then answer the following questions.

1. How many acres of land does Don Anselmo own in total?

   ____

2. What is the total length of his land in feet?

   ____

3. What is the total width of his land in feet?

   ____

4. What is the area of one acre in square feet ? (area = length × width)

   ____

5. Don Anselmo is selling eight acres of land for $1,200. How many dollars is that per acre?

   ____

6. How much were the Americans willing to pay Don Anselmo for the two pieces of property combined?

   ____

"Raymond's Run" by Toni Cade Bambara

Career Connection: Athletic Coach

Squeaky is the fastest runner in her neighborhood, and she makes a real effort to train herself for her races. She might be an even faster runner, however, if she had a track coach to guide her training.

Athletic coaches can help make the difference between a good athlete and a great one. They teach beginners the fundamentals of a sport, lead athletes through a season, and help world champions sharpen their skills. Coaches and instructors also help amateurs who simply want to increase their personal enjoyment of a sport or improve their exercise routine. Coaches can be found guiding teams and individuals at the professional and Olympic levels, at schools and colleges, and even at local fitness centers, ice rinks, and swimming pools.

The nature of the work of all athletic coaches is to teach. As a result, they must be knowledgeable in their respective sports, keep up with the latest procedures and techniques, and develop an effective teaching method to share the information with their athletes. Coaches at all levels must also be concerned with safety, ensuring that each athlete knows the proper methods of using equipment and maximizing performance without causing injury.

Athletic coaches at public and private schools are usually required to have a bachelor's degree from an accredited college or university. Sports instructors may not have a college or university degree, but they are usually skillful players of a particular sport. If you are considering a career as an athletic coach or instructor, a great way to start preparing is to participate in sports now.

A. DIRECTIONS: Use the information on the page and your own knowledge and experience to answer the following questions.

1. What are some of the duties of a middle school athletic coach?

   ____

   ____

2. What are some of the job opportunities for coaches and sports instructors?

   ____

   ____

3. In your opinion, what personality traits should a coach have to be successful at his or her job?

   ____

   ____

B. DIRECTIONS: Imagine you are the principal of a large middle school looking to hire an athletic coach. List four questions you would ask an applicant in an interview. Then trade papers with a classmate and answer each other's questions. Do you qualify for the job?

____

____

____

____

Unit 3: Quest for Justice

"Paul Revere's Ride" by Henry Wadsworth Longfellow

Cultural Connection: Heroes

Paul Revere is only one name on a long list of American heroes. Heroes are people whose actions are inspiring and noble and who possess qualities we admire. Our novels, stories, and poems are filled with the deeds of these people, providing examples of courage and lessons in how to overcome difficulties and rise to challenges.

We also have heroes in our everyday lives—the firefighter who risks his life to rescue an infant from a burning building, the driver who stops to help a woman injured in an automobile accident, and the quarterback with the surest throwing arm in the National Football League. A closer look at the heroes in our society reveals a lot about ourselves—what we care about and why.

A. DIRECTIONS: Use your own knowledge and experience of our culture to answer the following questions.

1. What are some character traits common to American heroes?

   ____

   ____

2. Why, do you think, there are more male than female heroes depicted in American history?

   ____

   ____

3. Do we make heroes of artists, scholars, physicians, or scientists? Why or why not?

   ____

   ____

4. Do you think it is important for a society to have heroes? Why or why not?

   ____

   ____

5. Do you think our idea of heroism will change in the next 100 years? Why or why not?

   ____

   ____

B. DIRECTIONS: Think of someone you consider to be a hero. This person may be famous or someone known only to you. Describe this person's heroic qualities.

____

____

____

____

____

"Always to Remember: The Vision of Maya Ying Lin" by Brent Ashabranner

Humanities Connection: Fine Art

Maya Lin competed with over 1,400 other entrants to design the Vietnam Veterans Memorial. When the board of directors of the Southern Poverty Law Center (SPLC) in Montgomery, Alabama decided they wanted a civil rights memorial, they called every Lin in the New York City phone book looking for Maya. They knew exactly who they wanted to design their memorial.

The SPLC was founded in 1971 to protect and advance the legal rights of minorities and poor people, and it remains one of the nation's leading civil rights organizations. Maya, inspired by the historical significance of the civil rights movement, agreed to design the monument. In researching the background of the civil rights movement, she came across these words by Martin Luther King, Jr.: "We will not be satisfied until justice rolls down like waters, and righteousness like a mighty stream."

King used these words from the Bible in several of his speeches. The words inspired Maya to use water as a main design element of the monument. The plan was to memorialize those individuals who had been killed in the cause of marching for civil rights. The SPLC came up with 53 entries they wanted etched in stone. Maya decided to create a huge, twelve-foot disk, or table of granite and to inscribe the names around the perimeter. The entries would be listed in chronological order from 17 May 1954, the Supreme Court ruling outlawing school segregation, to 4 April 1968, the assassination of Martin Luther King, Jr.

A black granite wall behind the disk rising nine feet would be inscribed with the words that inspired Maya, "until justice rolls down like waters, and righteousness like a mighty stream." Water would flow down the wall and across the disk, touching each name in the timeline. The disk would be close to the ground so people could walk around it and touch the inscriptions.

A. DIRECTIONS: Use the information on the page to answer the following questions.

1. Which organization commissioned the civil rights memorial?

   ____

2. What is inscribed on the black granite wall of the memorial?

   ____

B. DIRECTIONS: Imagine you are designing your own monument or memorial for a person or group you admire. Answer the following questions.

1. Which group or individual would you honor and why?

   ____

2. What design considerations would be important in your memorial? Explain.

   ____

3. What would you want visitors to experience when visiting your memorial? Explain.

   ____

C. DIRECTIONS: If you wish, draw your design on a separate sheet of paper.

Unit 3: Quest for Justice

from **"The People, Yes"** by Carl Sandburg

Career Connection: How Jobs Change

In this section of "The People, Yes," Carl Sandburg summarizes many different tales. Looking at the types of jobs mentioned or implied in these stories, we can see that as our society has changed, so have the types of jobs that people perform. While a job may have existed at the time the tales were created, technological or other changes may have erased the need for the job.

A. DIRECTIONS: List eight jobs specifically stated or implied in the selection, the line in which the job is mentioned, and a general job description of the job. The first is done for you.

	Line #	Occupation	General Job Description
1.	1	Architect	Designs buildings
2.			
3.			
4.			
5.			
6.			
7.			
8.			

B. DIRECTIONS: Choose one job that may have been affected by technological changes in the past several years. Then use your own knowledge and experience and either library or online resources to answer these questions.

Choose one job to examine further: ____

1. What does the verse of the poem imply about the nature of this job?

   ____

   ____

2. How has the nature of the job changed since the poem was published in 1936?

   ____

   ____

   ____

   ____

   ____

   ____

   ____

   ____

   ____

from *Travels with Charley* by John Steinbeck

Career Connection: Travel Writer

Almost everyone dreams of traveling to someplace for a weekend or a vacation. Whether seeking a day trip or a worldwide tour, you'll find numerous magazines, books, Web sites, and special newspaper sections devoted to the many aspects of travel. A **travel writer** is someone who writes for this special niche in publishing. A travel writer must have a talent for writing, interviewing, and research. He or she must also have curiosity, flexibility, and organizational skills. To succeed in this field, a travel writer should be willing to experience a variety of places, people, and events.

DIRECTIONS: Imagine that you are a travel writer and that your editor has asked you to write about the cultural aspects of a capital city anywhere in the world. Select a city that is unfamiliar to you. Plan your visit and the subject you will write about by filling in the following information.

City: ____

1. Travel Plans

   - How I will get there (bus, car, train, ship, airplane, etc.): ____________________

   - Length of stay (day-trip, weekend, week, longer): ____________________

   - Where I will stay (motel, hotel, bed-and-breakfast, rented apartment, private home, other):

   ____

   ____

   - What I plan to visit (libraries, museums, historical sites, other): ____________________

   ____

   ____

2. People I intend to interview: ____

   ____

   ____

(Choose at least three from the following list or from your own ideas.)

orchestra director	theater director
chamber of commerce president	concert hall manager
artistic director of a dance company	mayor
sculptor	an interpretor
dancer	actor
bookstore owner	museum director

3. What resources can you use to research the restaurants in town and the type of food served in them? Name at least three.

   ____

   ____

4. You're ready to go. In addition to your personal belongings, what items should you pack in order to perform your job?

   ____

"Choice: A Tribute to Dr. Martin Luther King, Jr." by Alice Walker
"The New Colossus" by Emma Lazarus
"Ellis Island" by Joseph Bruchac
"Achieving the American Dream" by Mario Cuomo

Cross-Curriculum Connection: Math

Ellis Island, named for Samuel Ellis who owned it in the 1770s, served as the port of entry for immigrants coming to America from 1892 until 1954. During its peak years, Ellis Island processed some twelve million immigrants. They came from countries all over the world. Some were refugees of political persecution, others sought freedom from religious persecution, and all came seeking a better way of life. The many cultures and religions are a rich part of the American heritage. Today, Ellis Island is fully restored and serves as a public museum under the direction of the National Park Service. Where immigrants once waited to be medically examined, tested, and processed, their descendants now walk comfortably through the halls, learning about what their ancestors may have experienced.

A. DIRECTIONS: Answer the following questions.

1. Ellis Island processed immigrants from 1892 to 1954. How many years was it open?

   ____

2. If twelve million immigrants came through Ellis Island between 1892 and 1924, what was the average number of immigrants to pass through each year?

   ____

3. In the early 1900s the average cost of a steamship ticket for an immigrant was $30.00. If a ship held 1,500 passengers, how much money did the ship owner collect?

   ____

B. DIRECTIONS: Listed below are the numbers of immigrants from eight European countries who passed through Ellis Island between January 1892 and June 1897. Use these figures to answer the questions that follow.

Immigrants Who Passed Through Ellis Island January 1892–June 1897

Italy	2,502,310	Norway	226,278
Russia	1,893,542	Portugal	120,725
Germany	633,148	Spain	72,636
Ireland	520,904	Belgium	63,141

1. How many more immigrants came from Russia than from Spain?

   ____

2. What is the *total number* of immigrants to have passed through in this time period?

   ____

3. What is the *average number* of immigrants per year during this time period?

   ____

4. Which country on this list sent the third largest number of immigrants to the United States?

   ____

"A Ribbon for Baldy" by Jesse Stuart
"The White Umbrella" by Gish Jen

Cross-Curricular Connection: Science

The low-lying clouds surrounding Baldy provide the idea for the science project in "A Ribbon for Baldy." Clouds come in a variety of shapes and sizes. It's easy to identify the type of cloud simply by looking at it. Some clouds seem to resemble objects or people. All clouds, however, are made of ice crystals and/or water droplets that are suspended in the air. Examine the following chart that identifies the four major cloud categories.

Cloud Category	Example	Description
High	cirrus	thin, wispy, fingerlike appearance; some have curled-up ends; sheet-like; can cover sky although transparent; create a halo effect around sun or moon
Middle	altocumulus	puffy masses, one part is darker; scattered uniform, difficult to detect individual elements; diffuse
Low	nimbostratus	typically dark gray; can contain light to moderate rain or snow; low; dark to light gray; can appear in rows, patches, or round masses with streaks of clear sky in between; tops are flat
Vertical	fair weather cumulus	floating cotton, popcornlike with defined outline; can develop cauliflower-like appearance; dome-shaped top
	cumulonimbus	can be single towering shape or line of towers; can develop large thunderheads; contains all forms of precipitation

DIRECTIONS: Use the information above to complete each of the following sentences.

1. Fog surrounded Baldy's base in the story. Since fog is close to the ground, fog is in the

   _________________________________ cloud category.

2. A major snowstorm is predicted. Chances are that _____________________________ clouds
   are hanging overhead.

3. The "blue sky" kind of clouds in which you imagine seeing another shape or face are

   usually _________________________________ clouds.

4. If it is a gray and misty day, chances are the clouds are _________________________________.

5. Fingerlike clouds streaking across the sky are called _________________________________.

6. There is just enough cloud cover to make things seem gloomy. In spite of that, the sun

   looks to be wearing a halo. The clouds are probably _________________________________.

7. Clouds described with foodlike characteristics are _________________________________.

8. Two types of clouds that contain rain or snow are _________________________________ and

   _________________________________.

     Beyond Literature   **25**

"Those Winter Sundays" by Robert Hayden
"Taught Me Purple" by Evelyn Tooley Hunt
"The City Is So Big" by Richard García

Cultural Connection: The Work Week

In "Those Winter Sundays," the father does the same thing he does every morning of the week during cold weather: He rises early and builds a fire. In other words, he works on weekends. Increasingly, more and more people work on Saturdays and Sundays—some because they hold more than one job, others because businesses are open seven days a week, and still others because certain work, such as milking cows on a dairy farm, must be done every day.

There was a time twenty or thirty years ago when almost everyone had Saturday and Sunday off. Most stores closed early on Saturday and almost no business was conducted on Sunday. Of course, there were exceptions. Farmers, certain religious leaders, doctors and nurses, newspaper reporters, and entertainers are just a few of those who often worked on weekends. Today, the hectic pace of life requires more and more people to work at least part of each weekend. More and more shops, businesses, and services are open 24 hours a day, seven days a week.

A. DIRECTIONS: Use the information provided and your own knowledge and experience to answer the following questions.

1. List three jobs which have always required people to work on Saturdays and Sundays.

   ____

   ____

   ____

2. List two types of businesses that are open on Saturdays and Sundays in most parts of the United States.

   ____

   ____

3. List two occupations that are unlikely to require that someone work on a Saturday or a Sunday.

   ____

   ____

4. Some occupations require individuals to be on-call on weekends, meaning they may not have to work but should be ready to work if needed. Name two of these occupations.

   ____

   ____

B. DIRECTIONS: In your opinion, what has been gained and what has been lost by creating a culture in which many shops and businesses operate seven days a week? Write your answer on a separate sheet of paper.

"Lights in the Night" from *An American Childhood* by Annie Dillard

Cultural Connection: Shadow Puppets

We don't often pay attention to shadows, even though they follow us everywhere. In Annie Dillard's autobiographical story, shadows trigger her imagination. Shadows have played a significant role in storytelling in many cultures, for many purposes.

One of the most intriguing uses of shadows is in **puppetry.** Paper or leather cutouts, often intricate and richly colored, are held behind a light-colored cloth (called a *screen*) and manipulated with rods. There are usually no more than three rods for a puppet—one for the body and two for the arms. The legs swing freely, but a skilled puppeteer can control their movement. A light shines behind the screen, creating shadows of the puppets. With these simple materials, a shadow puppeteer can tell epic stories or hilarious comedies.

Most historians consider India to be the birthplace of shadow shows. Since 200 B.C. shadow puppetry has been used in India to present the Mahabharata and the Ramayana, two epics of wars, gods, demons, heroes, and kings. Shadow shows have traditionally been performed to pass the central mythical tales of a culture from one generation to the next, providing entertainment while teaching important historical and religious themes.

Shadow puppetry eventually spread, by way of conquest and trade, to countries such as Malaysia, Java (an Indonesian island), China, Egypt, and Turkey. These cultures also use shadow puppetry to convey their own religious and historical themes. Shadow shows in Indonesia are presented for weddings, births, deaths, and even to cure illness. In China, shadow puppets first represented spirits of the dead, which is why the screen is called the "Screen of Death."

In Indonesia all puppetry is called *wayang* (which means shadow) because Indonesians say that drama is the shadow of life. Shadow puppet performances, called *wayang-kulit,* usually last all night, and the *dalang,* or puppeteer, must have stamina as well as skill. The dalang usually adds music and vocals to the performance, often including stories, songs, jokes, and political and philosophical thoughts. The show may be set outside to allow people to come and go throughout the night.

DIRECTIONS: Write your answers to the following questions.

1. Why do you think shadow puppetry is popular in many cultures? Explain. ________________

   ____

   ____

2. Why do you think shadow puppet shows are usually performed at night? ________________

   ____

   ____

3. *Wayang-kulit* is the name of Indonesian shadow puppets, and *kulit* means "leather." What does *wayang* mean, and how does this translation apply to shadow puppets?

   ____

   ____

4. What is the role of the *dalang* in Indonesian society? ________________________________

   ____

5. Imagine you are presenting a shadow puppet play. What story would you tell your audience? Why did you choose your story? Write your answer on the back of this paper.

    Beyond Literature **27**

"What Stumped the Blue Jays" by Mark Twain
"Why Leaves Turn Color In the Fall" by Diane Ackerman

Community Connection: Community Action

In "Why Leaves Turn Color In the Fall," the author writes that after leaves change color and fall from their branches they become a rich humus and feed the growth of new plants.

Successful home gardeners have long known about composting autumn's leaves, which means to store leaves and other plant material in wire bins and control their decomposition to produce compost. Imagine that you are helping your school ecology club make a poisitive change in your neighborhood or community. You plan on beginning a community composting project to encourage the recycling of leaves. How would you go about launching and completing this recycling project?

DIRECTIONS: Use the following chart to determine the steps you need to plan a community composting project. Complete each section of the chart.

Community Project: Compost Project to Recycle Auntumn Leaves

Goal Statement

1. ____

Task List to Reach Goal

2. ____

3. ____

4. ____

5. ____

People Who Can Assist

6. ____

7. ____

8. ____

Progress Evaluated

9. ____

10. ____

Impact of the Project on Community

11. ____

____

____

____

____

"Los New Yorks" by Victor Hernández Cruz
"Southbound on the Freeway" by May Swenson
"The Story-Teller" by Mark Van Doren

Cross-Curricular Connection: Math

In "Southbound on the Freeway," visitors from outer space see automobiles as the dominant life form on Earth. If the visitors had arrived in 1900 they would have had a very different impression; only 8,000 vehicles were registered in the United States. In the short span of only one hundred years, cars, trucks, and roads have covered the planet. There are now over 200 million cars registered in the United States and over 600 million registered vehicles on the planet.

Table A: Automobiles Registered in the United States

Year	Number	Year	Number	Year	Number
1900	8,000	1925	17,481,000	1970	89,243,557
1905	77,400	1930	23,034,753	1980	121,600,843
1910	458,377	1940	27,465,826	1990	143,549,627
1915	2,332,426	1950	40,339,077	1994	133,929,662
1920	8,131,522	1960	61,671,390	1995	136,066,045

Table B: Vehicles Registered Worldwide

Year	Number
1960	126,954,817
1970	246,367,545
1980	411,112,525
1990	582,981,777
1993	617,087,061

A. DIRECTIONS: Use Table A to answer the following questions.

1. How many automobiles were registered in 1905? _______________________________

   In 1990? _______________________________

2. How many more cars were there in 1920 than in 1910? _______________________________

3. What was the increase in the number of registered cars from 1950 to 1980? _____________

4. During which time period was there a decrease in the number of registered cars? ________

B. DIRECTIONS: Use Table B to answer the following questions.

1. What was the increase in registered vehicles from 1960 to 1993? _______________________

2. Which decade saw the greatest increase in vehicle registration? _______________________

   What was the increase? _______________________________

3. Do you think the world production of cars will increase or decrease during the first decade of the twenty-first century? Give your reasons. _______________________________

   ____

   ____

   ____

4. Has the increase in the number of cars been beneficial or detrimental? Give your reasons.

   ____

   ____

   ____

"The Adventure of the Speckled Band" by Sir Arthur Conan Doyle

Career Connection: Detective

When Sherlock Holmes solved the case of the speckled band, he showed resourcefulness, intelligence, tenacity, logical thinking, and the desire to help people. These are all characteristics of a good police detective. Detectives are the men and women of local police departments, state police agencies, and the Federal Bureau of Investigation (FBI) who gather information necessary to solve crimes.

After a crime has been committed, detectives gather information from the uniformed police officers who respond to the crime and from evidence technicians gathering physical evidence from the scene. Detectives talk to any victims or witnesses, and they interview anyone with possible information about the crime. A detective must be very organized and able to correlate information from many different sources. He or she must also be skilled at judging people's characters when questioning, interviewing, and observing witnesses and suspects. Many colleges and universities offer degrees in criminal justice for people who wish to enter this challenging field.

A. DIRECTIONS: Use information from the story to answer the following questions.

1. What was Holmes's first opportunity to use his detective skill for logical reasoning?

____

____

2. Which detective skill did Holmes employ during his first meeting with Miss Stoner?

____

3. What physical evidence did Holmes first examine at the house of Dr. Royloft?

____

____

4. What task of a successful police detective did Holmes perform when entering Miss Stoner's room?

____

____

B. DIRECTIONS: Use the information on this page and your own knowledge and experience to answer these questions.

1. What do you think is the most important characteristic of a good police detective? Give your reasons.

____

____

2. Which school subjects are important in preparing for a career as a detective? Explain your reasoning.

____

____

____

"A Glow in the Dark" by Gary Paulsen
"Mushrooms" by Sylvia Plath
"Southern Mansion" by Arna Bontemps
"The Bat" by Theodore Roethke

Cross-Curricular Connection: Science

In "A Glow in the Dark," the author describes a tree trunk that gives off a mysterious light. The noun *bioluminescence* means "the production of light by living organisms." Many plants and animals have the ability to produce their own light, such as the firefly. A firefly is really a flying beetle, and both the males and females flash light to attract mates. The males of a firefly species flash a certain pattern of light, and the female responds with her own pattern. Each different species has its own pattern of light. The light is created in light organs on the underside of their bodies, where chemical reactions inside living cells and tissue generate the light. On warm summer nights many North American backyards are scenes of flashing bioluminescence.

Fireflies may seem bright, but they are not the champions of creating light. The gold medal goes to the flashlight fish, which generates the brightest light of any living organism. This small 3.5-inch fish lives in dark crevices in coral reefs in the Indian Ocean. It has a small light organ just below its eye which holds billions of luminescent bacteria that feed on the blood of the fish. The bacteria actually create the light. The fish swim in large schools and attract prey with the light, which can be seen from 100 feet away.

Below 1,000 meters there are deep sea animals which make their home in complete darkness at temperatures near freezing and with pressures that would crush a human. Bioluminescence is widespread among these creatures, serving to lure prey, attract mates, and (possibly) communicate. Many species of fish, along with shrimp, squid, marine worms, and some jellyfish create their own light. The phosphorescent seas of the tropics are caused by marine algae flashing their light.

There are even luminous mushrooms common in tropical forests, often growing in rotted wood. Their light may attract insects, helping to spread their spores and aid in reproduction upon the forest floor.

DIRECTIONS: Answer the following questions on the lines provided.

1. What is the definition of bioluminescence?____

2. What is unique about the light of the flashlight fish? _______________________________

____

3. Why do you think that many animals living at great ocean depths are bioluminescent?

____

4. What is unique about the light of the firefly? ______________________________________

____

5. In "A Glow in the Dark," the main character learns that the tree stump was glowing because of phosphorus in the wood. What else might have caused a rotted tree stump to glow in the dark? ____

____

6. Would you have a reaction similar to that of the main character if you encountered eerie, glowing light while hiking in the woods at night? Explain. _________________________

____

                                                    Beyond Literature **31**

"The Tell-Tale Heart" by Edgar Allan Poe

Career Connection: Set Designer

A suspense story such as "The Tell-Tale Heart" is scary, in part, because of its setting, or the time and place of the action. Edgar Allan Poe's description of the darkened room, shadows, and creaky flooring creates an atmosphere of tension. In movies and plays, a **set designer** creates the proper mood, or atmosphere, through the selection and arrangement of scenery, props, and lighting. The set designer can do this on a stage, on location, or in a studio.

Imagine yourself as the set designer of a horror film. Your set design will provide moviegoers their first frightening glimpse of where the action will take place. You must consider the setting, the props, and the lighting.

A. DIRECTIONS: Design your set by providing details in each of the following areas. Make your descriptions as specific as possible.

Setting: Describe the location where the action will take place. (Outside/inside; forest/basement; kitchen/attic, and so forth)

____

____

____

Props: Describe some specific items in the scene. (Rusty wheelbarrow, torn couch, area rug, vase of flowers, and so forth)

____

____

____

Lighting: Describe how the scene will be illuminated. (Moonlight, lamplight, direct sunlight, shadows, and so forth)

____

____

____

B. DIRECTIONS: Think of a movie that especially scared or delighted you. Describe the most memorable scene in detail, noting the setting, props, and lighting.

____

____

____

____

____

____

____

____

Name ____ Date ____________________

"Hamadi" by Naomi Shihab Nye

"The Day I Got Lost" by Isaac Bashevis Singer

Study Skills: Map Reading

Professor Schlemiel in "The Day I Got Lost" needed a map to show him where he lived and how to get there. Maps not only help you find your destination but also teach you about places you may never have the chance to visit.

This map shows a section of our nation's capital, Washington, D.C.

DIRECTIONS: Fill in the blanks of the following statements with one of these directions: *north, south, east, west, northeast, southeast, northwest,* and *southwest.* Use the map to help you locate the sights.

1. The Washington Monument is _______________________________ of the White House.

2. The National Archives Building is _______________________________ of Ford's Theater.

3. The White House is due _______________________________ of the Treasury Department.

4. The Natural History Museum lies _______________________________ and _______________________________ of the American Art Museum.

5. The Federal Bureau of Investigation (FBI) building is _______________________________ of the Air and Space Museum.

6. The National Gallery of Art is _______________________________ of the Washington Monument.

7. The National Aquarium is _______________________________ of the U.S. Holocaust Museum and _______________________________ of the area known as The Ellipse.

8. Directly _______________________________ of the Old Executive Office Building and _______________________________ of the Washington Monument are both the White House and the Treasury Department.

"The Finish of Patsy Barnes" by Paul Laurence Dunbar
"Tears of Autumn" by Yoshiko Uchida

Study Skills: Making an Outline

"Tears of Autumn" introduces you to Hana when her journey to a new land is about to end and her new life is about to begin. She reflects on how she arrived at this moment and what propelled her toward this new adventure. In some way, Hana had very little to do with the final outcome. All she did was suggest to her uncle that she be the one to go to America to marry Taro Takedo. From that moment until her meeting with her future husband in America, much happened outside of Hana's personal control.

The steps others take on Hana's behalf help Hana get to America. These steps can be organized into an outline, a method used to show the essential features or main aspects of something. Outlines help you to organize information and to reinforce the main points you want to make in a composition or a speech. Making an outline can be especially helpful when you want to break down large and complex amounts of material into more understandable parts.

A. DIRECTIONS: Provide the following information to help you outline "Tears of Autumn."

1. List two characters that play an active role in shaping Hana's future.

____

____

2. List two actions that each character takes to help Hana achieve her new life.

____

____

____

3. List two details to support each of the character's actions.

____

____

____

B. DIRECTIONS: Use the information above to fill in the outline. Answers to the first question provide the two topics. Answers to the second question provide the two subtopics. Answers to the third question provide the supporting details.

Topic I. ____

  Subtopic A. ____

    Supporting details 1. ____

                   2. ____

Topic II. ____

  Subtopic A. ____

    Supporting details 1. ____

                   2. ____

Name ____ Date _________________________

"The Medicine Bag" by Virginia Driving Hawk Sneve
"The Story-Teller" by Saki

Community Connection: Parks

The man in "The Story-Teller" captures the children's interest by telling a story about an imaginary park filled with trees, ponds, and birds. In "The Medicine Bag," Grandpa leaves his reservation in South Dakota—a state famous for the Badlands National Park that comprises thousands of acres of shale and sandstone.

Parks come in all shapes and sizes and can be found in urban, suburban, and rural settings. Some are created and designed, such as Central Park in New York City. Some are wilderness areas, such as the Badlands National Park. Others are created around and about places of historic interest such as Gettysburg National Military Park and Mount Rushmore National Memorial.

The National Park Service, a bureau of the federal government's Department of the Interior, administers, protects, and maintains the parks for public appreciation and recreation. The National Park Service may build roads, trails, campgrounds, or provide forest management services. Each national park has a resident superintendent assisted by park rangers, naturalists, or historians to lead programs explaining the significance of the park. Local and state governments are responsible for city, county or state parks.

In all their forms, parks are places of community. Neighborhood parks provide opportunities for us to gather with friends or family. Wilderness-area parks allow us to congregate amidst the beauty and power of our natural landscape. Parks of historic interest bring us together to foster understanding of our national heritage.

A. DIRECTIONS: List three characteristics of each type of park under the headings below. The first entry is done for you.

Type of Park	Landscape	Natural Inhabitants	Activities	Facilities
Neighborhood	Paved area	Squirrels	Ball playing	Basketball net
	_________	_________	_________	_________
	_________	_________	_________	_________
Wilderness	_________	_________	_________	_________
	_________	_________	_________	_________
	_________	_________	_________	_________
Historic	_________	_________	_________	_________
	_________	_________	_________	_________
	_________	_________	_________	_________

B. DIRECTIONS: Describe a park you know or one you imagine. Explain how you might spend a day there. Include details of landscape, natural inhabitants, activities, and facilities. Then describe how spending a day in your park can help you gain a sense of community. Write your description on a separate sheet of paper.

"Animal Craftsmen" by Bruce Brooks

Cross-Curricular Connection: Science

In "Animal Craftsmen," author Bruce Brooks marvels at the ability of wasps and other creatures to design and construct perfect homes for themselves. Many animals possess a natural gift for building a protective and practical shelter. In many cases, animals face threats not only from other animals but also from people. In order for animals to survive, they need to have shelters that humans respect and help protect. For animals that are pets, people can provide help by creating a safe and secure environment in the home. For untamed animals, people can help by respecting the creatures' territories.

A. DIRECTIONS: Choose an animal that lives in the wild. Use an encyclopedia or other library reference to find out about the animal's specific needs. Then answer the questions below.

Animal: ____

1. What kind of climate does the animal require? Explain.

   ____

   ____

2. In what geographical location does the animal best survive? Explain.

   ____

   ____

3. What materials does the animal require to build its shelter? Explain.

   ____

   ____

4. What foods does the animal need? Explain.

   ____

   ____

5. What other requirements does the animal have for its survival? Explain.

   ____

   ____

6. In what ways can people show respect for the animal and its home? Explain.

   ____

   ____

B. DIRECTIONS: On the back of this paper, design a home for the animal of your choice. Before creating your design, take into consideration all the information you supplied above.

from *One Writer's Beginnings* by Eudora Welty

"Baseball" by Lionel G. García

Study Skills: Outlining

One Writer's Beginnings and "Baseball" are each based on the author's recollections of childhood. Eudora Welty recalls her misconceptions about the moon. Lionel García describes the unique variety of baseball that he and his friends played as kids. You may have childhood memories of special things you learned and games you played. Now that you are older, you have the opportunity to create a new game for young children to play. You can explain the game in the form of an outline.

DIRECTIONS: Working independently or with a partner, create a new game for children. Complete the outline below with information that children will need to know in order to play the game.

I. Name of Game: ____

II. Equipment or materials needed to play

    A. ____

    B. ____

    C. ____

III. Objective or goal

    ____

    ____

IV. Procedures (steps) for playing

    A. ____

    B. ____

    C. ____

    D. ____

    E. ____

    F. ____

V. Special rules

    A. ____

    B. ____

    C. ____

    D. ____

    E. ____

    F. ____

Beyond Literature **37**

Unit 7: Nonfiction

"Hokusai: The Old Man Mad About Drawing" by Stephen Longstreet
"Not to Go With the Others" by John Hersey

Media Connection: Film Documentary

In these biographies, the authors, Stephen Longstreet and John Hersey, describe highly unusual individuals. Longstreet depicts Katsushika Hokusai as a gifted Japanese artist who is noted for his unique and ever-changing styles of painting. Hersey describes Frantizek Zaremski as a tough World War II survivor whose remarkable instincts enable him to stay alive by not following others. It is easy to imagine how a documentary about the life of either Hokusai or Zaremski might make a gripping film.

Not everyone in life becomes the subject of a biography or documentary. Yet every individual is unique. Although you may have some of the same characteristics as relatives and friends, the totality of your traits and habits makes you unlike anyone else. If you were to make a film documentary about your life, you would want to emphasize those aspects of your character that make up your unique personality.

DIRECTIONS: Choose someone you admire and know well to be a subject of a film documentary. This person may be a friend, family member, teacher, religious or community leader or another person you know and admire. Use the lines provided to plan your documentary.

Name of Subject: ____

1. Name at least three special personality traits of this person to be highlighted in the documentary.

   ____

   ____

   ____

2. Name three incidents from this person's life to illustrate his or her individual personality.

   ____

   ____

   ____

3. Name three of the subject's family members, friends, or associates to be interviewed in the documentary. Explain briefly what you intend to ask each of these people.

   a. ____

   ____

   b. ____

   ____

   c. ____

   ____

4. Explain how you intend to organize your documentary. (For example, you might decide to present information in chronological order, or the order in which events took place in the person's life.)

   ____

   ____

"Debbie" by James Herriot

"Forest Fire" by Anaïs Nin

Workplace Skills: Acting Responsibly

In each of the two selections, the author deals in some way with matters of proper behavior. In "Debbie," Mrs. Ainsworth apologizes to Mr. Herriot for asking him to come out on Christmas Day to tend to her sick cat. In "Forest Fire," a news reporter grows annoyed with Anaïs Nin when she chooses to salvage her diaries instead of her clothing, as the fire threatens to spread.

In your own life, there will be many times when you must make choices regarding appropriate behavior. It may not always be easy to know or decide on the proper way to behave.

DIRECTIONS: Describe what you would do in each situation below. Explain your reasoning.

1. You checked out a library book that is now overdue. You still need the book for a report. The library has called to say that another person wants to check out the same book and that there is no other copy. What do you do?

____

____

____

____

2. Your best friends have gone somewhere that their parents have told them not to go. Now your friends want you to tell their parents that they spent the time at your house. You know they will get in serious trouble if their parents discover where they really were. What do you do?

____

____

____

____

3. You eat at a restaurant where the waiter was slightly rude to you and your friend. After the meal, you still feel obligated to leave a tip. What do you do?

____

____

____

____

4. You have a midterm examination in history but you do not start studying until the night before the exam. At 11 P.M., you realize that you do not have the list of questions the teacher provided to help you review. Your friend could help but it's late to call. What do you do?

____

____

____

                                          Beyond Literature **39**

Unit 7: Nonfiction

"The Trouble with Television" by Robert MacNeil
"The American Dream" by Martin Luther King, Jr.

Cultural Connection: Television and Society

In his essay, Robert MacNeil is critical of television and of viewers who watch it excessively. While he believes that television may be fine as entertainment, he is concerned about its long-term effects on American viewers and their values. In Martin Luther King, Jr.'s essay, the author is also concerned with America's values.

Both MacNeil and King might agree that television does not reflect society as it really exists. You may or may not agree with this view. Now you have the opportunity to defend or criticize television as a mirror of the society that you live in.

A. DIRECTIONS: Explain why television does or does not realistically reflect each of the following aspects of our society. Consider all types of television programming from documentaries and news reports to television movies and situation comedies.

1. teenagers

____

____

____

2. school

____

____

____

3. family

____

____

____

B. DIRECTIONS: Imagine you are given the opportunity to develop a new weekly television show that will reflect society as it really exists. Describe the type of show you want to present.

____

____

____

____

____

____

____

____

____

____

***The Diary of Anne Frank,* Act I** by Frances Goodrich and Albert Hackett

Cross-Curricular Connection: Art

A memorial serves to keep the memory of a person alive. Many sculptures are designed as memorials. The Lincoln Memorial in Washington, D.C., is a realistic sculpture of Abraham Lincoln. Because the sculpture is realistic, anyone who sees it is instantly reminded of Abraham Lincoln.

Memorials, however, are not always realistic. Some memorials are designed to keep alive the ideals a person stood for or to remind others of the person's remarkable and admirable characteristics.

DIRECTIONS: Use the questions below to help you plan a sculpture that honors Anne Frank. Then create a message for a plaque on your sculpture.

1. What impressed you most about Anne Frank? Explain.

   ____

   ____

   ____

2. What would you like people to know about Anne Frank? Explain.

   ____

   ____

   ____

3. What would you like people to remember about Anne Frank? Explain.

   ____

   ____

   ____

4. How could you represent these ideas in a sculpture? Explain.

   ____

   ____

   ____

5. Use the remaining lines on this page to draft the message that the plaque on your sculpture will contain. ____

   ____

   ____

   ____

   ____

   ____

   ____

   ____

Unit 8: Drama

The Diary of Anne Frank, Act II by Frances Goodrich and Albert Hackett

Humanities Connection: Philosophy

In addition to raising many ethical and moral questions, _The Diary of Anne Frank_ presents various philosophies of life as expressed through Anne and other characters. For example, Anne's beliefs about family, strangers, love, and other issues are made apparent through what she says and writes in her diary. Her most powerful philosophy is stated at the end of the play: "In spite of everything, I still believe that people are really good at heart." You may or may not agree with that philosophy, based on your own life experiences. You may also agree or disagree with other philosophies expressed in the play.

DIRECTIONS: For each statement from the play, express your own personal philosophy. Support your views with examples, facts, and other details.

1. MR. FRANK. "We won't be living here according to regulations." Under what conditions, if any, are people justified in breaking the law?

   ____

   ____

2. MRS. FRANK. "You complain that I don't treat you like a grownup. But when I do, you resent it." How much should children be treated like grownups, if at all?

   ____

   ____

3. MRS. VAN DAAN. "It's nothing to be ashamed of, to have a little girl friend." At what age do you feel people are ready to have boyfriends or girlfriends? Why?

   ____

   ____

4. MR. VAN DAAN. "There's so little food as it is . . . and to take in another person . . ." Should people share what they have if it will create a shortage for themselves?

   ____

   ____

5. MR. VAN DAAN. " . . . cat looks better than any of us. Out he goes tonight!" Should animals always be treated with the same regard as humans? Explain.

   ____

   ____

6. ANNE. "You grownups have had your chance! But . . . we're trying to hold onto some kind of ideals." Do younger people deserve more out of life than older people?

   ____

   ____

7. ANNE. "In spite of everything, I still believe that people are really good at heart." Do you believe that, basically, all people are good at heart? Why or why not?

   ____

   ____

"The Secret Heart" by Robert P. Tristram Coffin

Cross-Curricular Connection: Science

In "The Secret Heart," the heart is an image. The heart is a universal symbol of love and affection.

Below is a diagram of how the human heart actually functions.

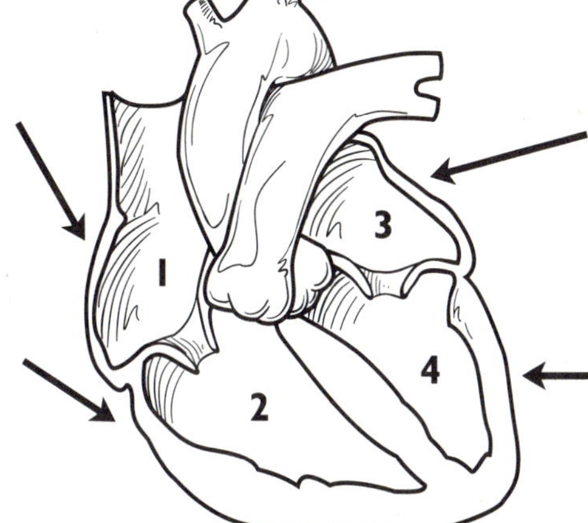

DIRECTIONS: Refer to the diagram of the heart to answer these questions.

1. When blood from the body enters the heart, where does it go first?

____

2. This blood that enters the heart has something in it that is not good for the body. What is it?

____

3. What is the purpose of the right ventricle?

____

4. After the blood picks up oxygen from the lungs, where does it go?

____

5. What part of the heart pumps the oxygen-rich blood to the rest of the body?

____

Unit 9: Poetry

"The Wreck of the Hesperus" by Henry Wadsworth Longfellow
"The Centaur" by May Swenson

Study Skills: Reading Graphic Organizers

Beaufort Scale of Wind Force			
Beaufort number	**Knots (mph)**	**Description**	**Effect at sea**
0	less than 1	Calm	Sea is like a mirror.
1	1–3 (1–3)	Light air	Ripples that look like scales are formed but without foam crests.
2	4–6 (4–7)	Light breeze	Small wavelets appear; crests look glassy but do not break.
3	7–10 (8–12)	Gentle breeze	Large wavelets appear. Crests begin to break. Foam looks glassy, perhaps with scattered whitecaps.
4	11–16 (13–18)	Moderate breeze	Small waves appear, becoming longer; there are fairly frequent whitecaps.
5	17–21 (18–24)	Fresh breeze	Moderate waves arise, taking a longer form; many white caps (with some chance of spray).
6	22–27 (25–31)	Strong breeze	Large waves begin to form; whitecaps are everywhere (probably with some spray).
7	28–33 (32–38)	Moderate gale (high wind)	Sea heaps up and white foam from breaking waves begins to be blown in streaks along the direction of the wind.
8	34–40 (39–46	Fresh gale	Moderately high, longer waves appear; edges of crests break. Foam is blown in direction of the wind.
9	41–47 (47–54)	Strong gale	High waves appear. Sea begins to roll. Spray may affect visibility.
10	48–55 (55–63)	Storm	Very high waves with long crests. Sea looks white. Rolling of the sea becomes heavy. Visibility is affected.
11	55–63 (64–73)	Violent storm	Exceptionally high waves. (Small and medium–sized ships might be lost to view behind the waves.) The sea is covered with foam and froth. Visibility is affected.
12	above 63 (73)	Hurricane	The air is filled with foam and spray. Sea is completely white with a driving spray. Visibility is very seriously affected.

DIRECTIONS: Put yourself in the place of the skipper in "The Wreck of the Hesperus." When you brought your daughter onto the schooner, the weather was probably good for sailing. As the evening went on, however, the weather changed. Describe those changes, as seen through the skipper's eyes. Refer to the chart above as you try to imagine what the skipper saw. Write your description on a sheet of paper.

"Harlem Night Song" by Langston Hughes
"Blow, Blow, Thou Winter Wind" by William Shakespeare
"love is a place" by E. E. Cummings
"January" by John Updike

Career Connection: Meteorologist

Meteorologists are scientists who study the atmosphere. The best known application of their knowledge is forecasting the weather. Other applications for this knowledge are air-pollution control, agriculture, air and sea transportation, and defense. In addition, meteorologists study trends in Earth's atmosphere, such as global warming and the thinning of the ozone layer.

Most meteorologists predict the weather. They do this by studying information on air pressure, temperature, humidity, and wind speed. With this information, they can make short- and long-range weather forecasts. They obtain data from weather satellites, weather radar, and remote sensors and observers all over the world. Professionally, these meteorologists are called *operational meteorologists.*

Some meteorologists work in research. For example, *physical meteorologists* study the chemical and physical properties of the atmosphere. They also study how clouds, rain, snow, and other weather conditions are formed. Other meteorologists, called *synoptic meteorologists,* develop new tools for forecasting the weather. Still others, called *climatologists,* collect and analyze past records of the weather in specific areas. Their studies are used to design buildings, plan heating and cooling systems, and plan agricultural use of the land.

If you want to become a meteorologist, you will need a bachelor's degree with courses in meteorology, advanced math, physics, statistics, and computer science, among other things. You can start now by studying physical science, math, and computers.

DIRECTIONS: Refer to the information on this page to answer the following questions.

1. What do operational meteorologists do?

   ____

   ____

2. What do physical meteorologists do?

   ____

   ____

3. What do synoptic meteorologists do?

   ____

   ____

4. What do climatologists do?

   ____

   ____

5. What kind of training is necessary for a person who wants to be a meteorologist?

   ____

   ____

Unit 9: Poetry

"Ode to Enchanted Light" by Pablo Neruda
Two Haiku by Bashō and Moritake
"She Dwelt Among the Untrodden Ways" by William Wordsworth
"Harriet Beecher Stowe" by Paul Laurence Dunbar
from "John Brown's Body" by Stephen Vincent Benét
"400-Meter Free Style" by Maxine Kumin

Cross-Curricular Connection: Science

The haiku by Moritake is about a butterfly. The adult butterfly is the final stage in this insect's life cycle, which is illustrated below. This dramatic change in form is known as *metamorphosis.*

DIRECTIONS: Read the following information, and then identify and add captions to each stage of a butterfly's life in the illustration.

The Lifecycle of the Butterfly

The adult butterfly lays its eggs on the leaves of a plant. In a few days, the eggs will hatch and a caterpillar will emerge. The main job of the caterpillar is to eat, for it is storing food for the next stage. As it eats, it grows, but its skin does not. When the skin is stretched to the limit, the caterpillar spins a silken pad and attaches itself to it. The caterpillar then remains still for a few days while it develops new skin. When it is ready, the caterpillar sheds the old skin, or molts, and can continue growing inside its new, looser skin.

When the caterpillar reaches maturity, it loses its appetite and begins to change. In a short time, it will stop eating altogether and look for a place from which to hang. Eventually, it will become translucent (almost clear) and hang suspended from a branch or a leaf, holding on by a button of silk spun from its own body.

Within 24 hours, the caterpillar will shed its caterpillar skin for the last time, and the chrysalis will emerge. The chrysalis is a hard shell that looks something like a leaf. Some species have a chrysalis that looks like a dead, dry leaf; others have a green chrysalis that looks like a living leaf. Either way, it blends in with the plant. Inside the chrysalis, the butterfly is forming.

When it is ready, the butterfly emerges from the chrysalis. Most butterflies feed on nectar from flowers and are active during the day. The main job of the adult butterfly is to mate and, for the females, to lay eggs and let the process begin all over again. The eggs are always laid on the kind of food that the caterpillar will eat. The life span of a butterfly ranges from a few days to as long as ten months, depending on the species. Most adults live from four to six weeks.

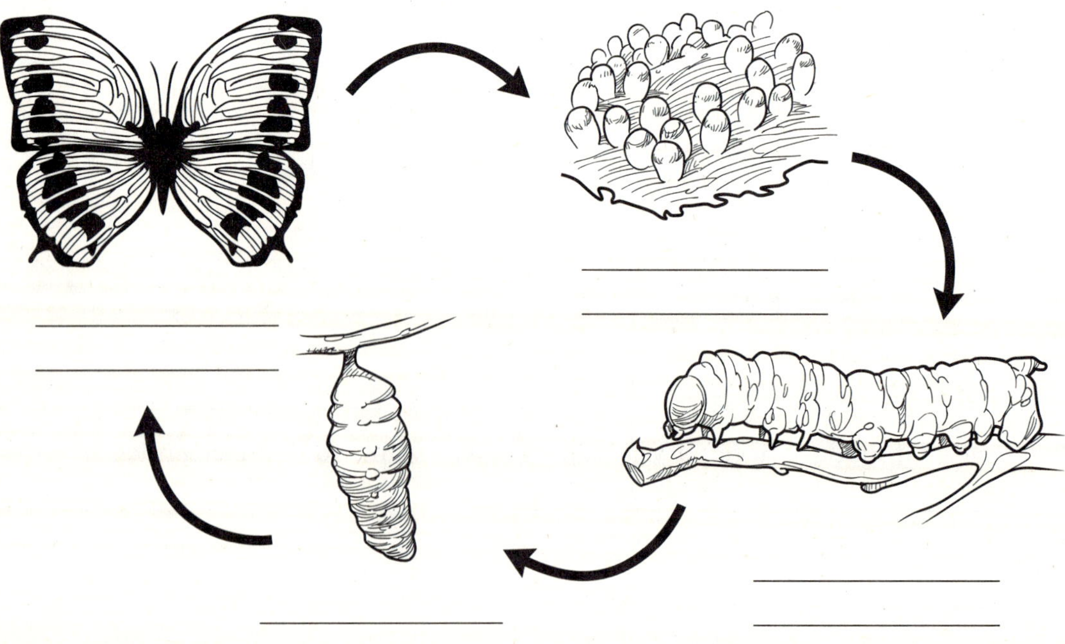

"Silver" by Walter de la Mare

"Forgotten Language" by Shel Silverstein

"Drum Song" by Wendy Rose

"If I can stop one Heart from breaking" by Emily Dickinson

Study Skills: Using a Graphic Organizer

Charts are useful because they display information in an organized, easy-to-read format. A chart lets you compare similar aspects of many different things.

DIRECTIONS: Practice using a graphic organizer by completing the chart below. Column 1 lists animals mentioned in the poems. Complete columns 2, 3, and 4. Then add your own heading to column 5, and complete it as well. If necessary, refer to a dictionary, encyclopedia, or other reference.

Animal	Body covering— (fur, feathers, scales, or other)	Number of legs	Number of wings	
dog				
dove				
mouse				
fish				
caterpillar				
starling				
housefly				
cricket				
turtle				
woodpecker				
snow hare				
owl				
robin				

"New World" by N. Scott Momaday
"Lyric 17" by José Garcia Villa
"For My Sister Molly Who in the Fifties" by Alice Walker

Cultural Connection: The Pulitzer Prize

Two of the poets in this grouping, N. Scott Momaday and Alice Walker, are winners of the Pulitzer Prize. The Pulitzer Prizes have been given since 1917 by Columbia University, based on recommendations by the Pulitzer Prize Board. There are fourteen prizes given each year for achievements in American journalism. Awards are also given in American letters, drama, and music. The letters categories are fiction, history, poetry, biography or autobiography, and general nonfiction. Although these awards have little monetary value in themselves, it is a great honor to receive one.

The prizes were the idea of Joseph Pulitzer, an American newspaper publisher. Pulitzer was born in Hungary in 1847 and immigrated to the United States. In 1878, Pulitzer became the owner and publisher of the *St. Louis Post-Dispatch,* and under his guidance, the newspaper became a success. In 1883, he bought the *New York World* and made it a great success, too. People liked his use of illustrations, news stunts, crusades against corruption, cartoons, and bold news coverage.

In 1890, Pulitzer suffered partial blindness, which kept him from political activity. Still, he continued to direct his papers. He gave money to establish what is now the Graduate School of Journalism at Columbia. His money also endowed the Pulitzer Prizes.

DIRECTIONS: Refer to the information above to answer these questions.

1. How did Joseph Pulitzer achieve success in America?

   ____

   ____

2. What stopped Joseph Pulitzer from continuing his political activity?

   ____

   ____

3. Which institution awards the Pulitzer Prizes?

   ____

4. Which board decides on the winners of the Pulitzer Prizes?

   ____

5. In which categories are the Pulitzer Prizes awarded?

   ____

6. Can a person who writes for a French newspaper win a Pulitzer Prize? Why or why not?

   ____

   ____

   ____

   ____

"The Dark Hills" by Edwin Arlington Robinson
"Incident in a Rose Garden" by Donald Justice

Study Skills: Using an Outline

An outline can help you organize ideas and information. When you write an outline, you group these ideas in an organized pattern that shows their order and their relationship to one another.

A. DIRECTIONS: Read the following essay to learn more about the flowers featured in "Incident in a Rose Garden." As you read, think about the major ideas of the essay and how they can be organized in outline form.

Taking Care of Roses

During the growing season, roses need a lot of water. If they don't get enough, their growth and blooming will slow down. Water deeply to be sure that the entire root system is moistened. The bigger the plant, the more water it will need. Basin flooding, or simply letting water from a hose flood the area around the roses, is one way to do it. Another way is to use a drip irrigation system. Still another way is to use overhead sprinkling. This last method is a good way to remove dust and freshen the foliage; it also helps control aphids and spider mites. A disadvantage to overhead sprinkling is that it sometimes encourages foliage diseases by keeping the foliage and air damp. If you decide to use overhead sprinkling, be sure to do it early in the day so the sun can dry off the foliage by nightfall.

Nutrients are necessary if you want healthy plants and beautiful roses. Apply fertilizers when a blooming period has come to an end and new growth period is just beginning. Dry commercial fertilizers, which are added to the soil, produce good results. Liquid fertilizers are good for smaller gardens in which roses are basin watered. Most liquid fertilizers can also be sprayed on rose leaves, which can absorb the nutrients right away.

Pest and disease control is usually needed during the growing season. Rose pests include aphids, spider mites, and thrips. You can use mechanical controls, such as hand-picking or a strong jet of water, to get rid of some of these pests. You can also release or encourage certain insects that will eat the pests. Other remedies include soaps and special oils. For problems such as mildew, rust, and black spot, you will probably have to use a chemical control.

B. DIRECTIONS: Complete the following outline on a separate sheet of paper.

Taking Care of Roses

A. Watering
  1. Basin flooding
  2.
  3.
    a. Advantages
      i.
      ii.
    b. Disadvantages
      i.

B. Nutrients
  1.
  2.

C. Pest and disease control
  1. Aphids, spider mites, thrips
    a. mechanical controls
      i.
      ii.
    b.
    c.
  2.

"Chicoria" by José Griego y Maestas and Rudolfo A. Anaya
"Brer Possum's Dilemma" by Jackie Torrence
"Why the Waves Have Whitecaps" by Zora Neale Hurston
"Coyote Steals the Sun and Moon," retold by Richard Erdoes and Alfonso Ortiz

Cross-Curricular Connection: Science

While Zora Neale Hurston's "Why the Waves Have Whitecaps" is a folktale, the story has basis in fact. Wind does cause waves to have whitecaps. When wind hits the water, the water is pushed into waves. The following diagram shows the chief characteristics of waves.

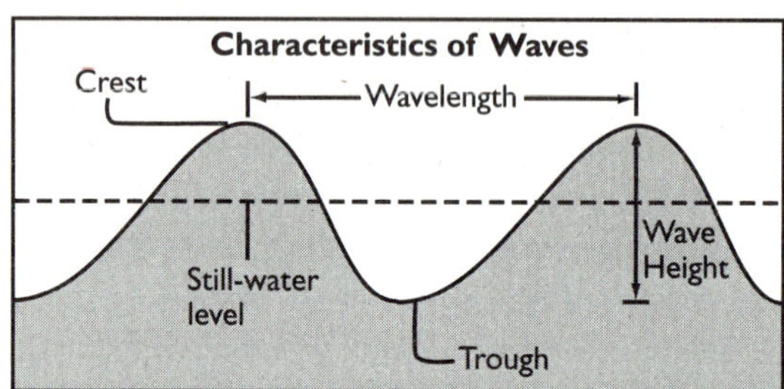

As the wind blows across the surface of the water, little ripples begin to form. When the wind gets stronger, the little ripples become larger waves. The size of a wave is determined by how fast the wind is blowing, the length of time the wind blows, and the distance the wind blows over the water. As each of these factors increases, the height of a wave increases. Some waves can become really huge. The largest surface wave ever measured occurred in the northern Pacific Ocean on February 7, 1933. At that time, a wind storm was sweeping over a stretch of water thousands of kilometers long. A ship in the United States Navy measured a wave at 34 meters high! (Such a wave would rise above a ten story building.)

It may look as if the water is moving along with the wave, but it is not. The wave carries the energy of the wind (or the tide or the current), but the water itself stays pretty much in the same place. As the energy of the wave passes, the particles of water move in a little circle. You can test this fact by placing a stick on the water to float as the waves pass by. You'll notice that it bobs up and down but stays in just about the same spot.

DIRECTIONS: Use the diagram and the information on the page to answer the following questions.

1. What is the high spot of a wave called? _______________________________________

2. What is the low spot of a wave called? _______________________________________

3. What is the distance between two crests or two troughs called? ___________________

4. What is the distance from the trough to the crest called? _______________________

5. What do you think would happen if wind came from more than one direction at once?

   ____

6. What do you think would happen to a boat on water that had small waves?

   ____

   ____

7. What would happen to a boat on water in which the waves got bigger and bigger?

   ____

   ____

"John Henry" Traditional
"Paul Bunyan of the North Woods" by Carl Sandburg
"Pecos Bill: The Cyclone" by Harold W. Felton
"Davy Crockett's Dream" by Davy Crockett

Workplace Skills: Goal Setting

Before you can accomplish anything, you must have goals. You can have short-term goals, such as learning to sing a certain song, or you can have long-term goals, such as becoming an accomplished musician. To achieve long-term goals, you have to set and achieve many short-term goals along the way.

A. DIRECTIONS: In the chart below, keep track of the goals of each hero and the steps he took to achieve those goals.

	Goal	Steps to Achieve Goal
John Henry		
Paul Bunyan		
Pecos Bill		
Davy Crockett		

B. DIRECTIONS: Think about the goals you have for yourself, or set some new ones. Use this chart to record some of these goals and the steps you plan to take to achieve them.

Goal	Steps to Achieve Goal

Unit 10: The American Folk Tradition

ANSWERS
Unit 1:   Coming of Age

"The Drummer Boy of Shiloh"
by Ray Bradbury

Cross-Curricular Connection: Social Studies (p. 1)

1. Confederacy side. We know from the story that the men knew there would be a battle on the following day. Since it was a surprise attack, the men on the Union side didn't know that fact.
2. It had to be Johnston because he was the one who was in command on the first day.
3. It was the first big battle of the Civil War, and it showed the North that the South would not give up easily.

"Charles" by Shirley Jackson

Career Connection: School Counselor (p. 2)

Sample responses:

A. 2. Immature. Usually by the age of four, a child can use correct grammar, and Laurie, age five, is still having trouble with double negatives.

3. Typical. It is normal for a child of Laurie's age to enjoy rhymes.

4. Immature. Laurie has quite an imagination but, like a typical four-year-old, he seems to have trouble distinguishing between fact and fantasy.

B. Students may say that their assessments indicate that Laurie's behavior is more immature than typical for a child his age. They may recommend some brief counseling to help Laurie accept the need for fair play and restraint. They may also suggest that Laurie have some extra help in grammar.

from *I Know Why the Caged Bird Sings* by Maya Angelou

Community Connection: Learning from Elders (p. 3)

A. Mrs. Bertha Flowers is well dressed, calm, well mannered, and graceful. She is a gentlewoman who appreciates good literature, language, and the art of communication. These qualities can help a protégé by exam-

ple. Sample answers for second part of chart: patience, knowledge about diving, ability to teach me how to dive, enthusiasm.

B. Sample answer: I would try to teach my protégé good manners. One lesson might be on the importance of writing thank-you notes. Sample paragraph: I would teach my protégé that it is important to write a thank-you note promptly when you receive a gift or enjoy someone's hospitality as a guest. The note does not have to be long— in fact, it should not be long. The important thing is to let the other person know how much you appreciated what he or she did for you. Even if you don't really like the gift or if you didn't have a good time at a party, you should still write a note to acknowledge that you appreciate the effort put forth by the other person.

"The Road Not Taken"
by Robert Frost
"All But Blind" by Walter de la Mare
"The Choice" by Dorothy Parker

Workplace Skills: Decision Making (p. 4)

Sample answer: The choices: to go out for baseball or get an after-school baby-sitting job.

Choice #1: baseball. Pros: fun, good exercise, can make new friends. Cons: takes a lot of time, no pay, might get injured. Choice #2: baby-sitting. Pros: can earn spending money, can earn money to save for college, can be useful to another family, can learn about child development, can do homework while earning money. Cons: sometimes kids are hard to handle, might have an emergency that could be scary, cuts into social life, cuts into time at home.

from "E-Mail from Bill Gates"
by John Seabrook

Study Skills: Using the Internet (p.5)

A. Suggested responses for each (search engine at www.yahoo.com)

1. iguana care pet
2. weather Portland Oregon

3. television listings guide

4. chemical element symbol

5. population New York City

6. Herman Melville

7. NBA team league

8. tooth care

B. Sample answer:

(Using www.yahoo.com). Keywords to find information on tooth care: Type "tooth care" in the box and click on search button. Scroll down the list of categories to Health:Medicine:Dentistry. Click on "Dental Consumer Advisor". Click on "Dental Health Facts". *(Please be aware that sites may have changed since we published this information. We strongly suggest that you supervise students as they access sites).*

"The Old Grandfather and His Little Grandson" by Leo Tolstoy
"Grandma Ling" by Amy Ling
"Old Man" by Ricardo Sánchez

Cultural Connection: Attitudes Toward Old Age (p. 6)

A. Sample answers:

1. Advertisement #1 is for a pain medicine. The picture shows an elderly woman gardening and smiling at the camera.

2. Advertisement #2 is for denture paste. The picture shows an elderly couple dancing. They are smiling at each other.

3. From these advertisements I conclude that you can be active and have a good time even if you are old.

B. Sample answers: In his eighties, Robert Frost wrote and read a poem at John Kennedy's presidential inauguration. In his seventies, John Glenn served as United States Senator and, at this printing, was expected to return to space as the world's oldest astronaut. In his nineties, Pablo Picasso turned to sculpture. In her nineties, O'Keefe continued to paint. In her eighties, Sojourner Truth continued to lecture.

"Poets to Come" by Walt Whitman
"Winter Moon" by Langston Hughes
"Ring Out, Wild Bells" by Alfred, Lord Tennyson

Cross-Curricular Connection: Science (p. 7)

A. 1. b; 2. d; 3. a; 4. c

B. My interest in becoming a doctor began to wane when I realized how much it would cost to complete medical school.

Unit 2:   Meeting Challenges

"Cub Pilot on the Mississippi" by Mark Twain

Workplace Skills: Conflict Resolution (p. 8)

Suggested responses:

1. Twain could begin by asking Brown how he could be of service rather than waiting quietly for orders. Twain could respectfully ask Mr. Brown how he might live up to Brown's expectations.

2. The plan does not seem to work because Brown continues to bully Twain and refuses to admit that Twain is doing his best.

3. Twain could ask the pilot George Ealer for his advice. He could tell the captain about the problem and request another duty for the remainder of the trip.

"The Secret" by Arthur C. Clarke

Workplace Skills: Acting Responsibly (p. 9)

Suggested responses:

1. People may be angry when they discover that their budget dollars are being spent in space and yet only a select few benefit by living longer on a more spacious planet. They may take away the funding for the UNSA because it doesn't benefit them. Or, they may push to set up human colonies in space as quickly as possible.

2. As a reporter, Cooper would fail in his responsibility to inform the public. He may feel guilty over this decision. If someone else reveals the secret instead, he would lose credibility when it was learned that he knew of the secret and chose to remain silent.

3. Students should provide a detailed answer that takes into account the consequences of the action.

"Harriet Tubman: Guide to Freedom"
by Ann Petry

Humanities Connection: Personal Courage (p. 10)

A. Sample responses:

2. Defending someone puts you out on a limb

3. Must overcome the fear of failure

4. By sticking to your principles and taking an unpopular stand, you run the risk of being called names or being shut out of groups

B. Students should be as specific as possible in pointing out the courageous aspects of the person's life. Sample response: a grandparent or great-grandparent who fled oppression or war in their homeland, took a chance on the unknown in the United States, and made a life despite poverty, discrimination, and so forth.

"Columbus" by Joaquin Miller
"Western Wagons"
by Stephen Vincent Benét
"The Other Pioneers"
by Roberto Félix Salazar

Media Connection: Documentary Film (p. 11)

Suggested responses:

1. Documentary film can reveal details such as personal mannerisms and speaking styles that written accounts cannot. A documentary film can provide a sense of immediacy with first-hand accounts and pictures of events as they happened.

2. Written accounts are easily portable and can be read anywhere, whereas films require equipment. Encyclopedias or textbooks provide an expert's summary or comments about an event or person while a film documentary may leave the viewer to draw his or her own conclusions.

3. a. Columbus: What would you have done if your crew had turned against you and wanted to return home? Explain a typical day on the ship.

   b. A teenage pioneer girl: What did you fear on the trail? What did you miss most back home? Explain a typical day on the journey.

   c. A Native American chief: What have you learned from these settlers and what have you taught them? What did you fear most about the settlers?

   d. A Mexican father: What do you hope this new land will provide for you and your children? Talk about the struggle of daily life in a desert climate.

4. Most likely fewer families would have headed west if they had seen a film of people starving on the trail, battling with Native Americans, or freezing in the mountains.

"Up The Slide" by Jack London

Cross-Curricular Connection: Physical Education (p. 12)

Suggested responses:

1. A climber may grow careless or too confident on an easy climb.

2. a. Bicycling: Strengthens legs

   b. Gymnastics: Increases flexibility

   c. Chin-ups: Strengthens arms

3. a. A climber would first shout "Rock" and then "Rope."

   b. A climber would shout "Climbing" and then "Slack."

   c. A climber would shout "Watch me."

"Thank You, M'am"
by Langston Hughes

Cross-Curricular Connection: Math (p. 13)

2. $.70 - $.20 = $.50 price increase; .50 divided by .20 = 2.50 × 100 = 250% inflation over 30 years

3. $1.34 - $.26 = $1.08 price increase; 1.08 divided by .26 = 4.15 × 100 = 415% inflation over 30 years

"Thank You, M'am"
by Langston Hughes
(continued)

4. $16,012 – $2,610 = $13,402 price increase; 13,402 divided by 2,610 = 5.13 × 100 = 513% inflation over 30 years

5. $123,000 – $12,675 = $110,325 price increase; 110,325 divided by 12,675 = 8.70 × 100 = 870% inflation over 30 years

"Flowers for Algernon"
by Daniel Keyes

Cross-Curricular Connection: Science (p. 14)

Suggested responses:

1. I think we should leave people's intelligence alone because the world needs people of different abilities.

2. Charlie liked learning and the experiment helped him learn more. One thing he discovered, however, was that people can be cruel. He remained an outsider because he was smarter than anyone else.

3. IQ tests might show where people are weakest in learning so that they can get the help they need.

4. IQ tests might not work with people of a culture different from the general population. They might label people rather than help them.

5. Both heredity and experience make up intelligence. If twins are separated at birth and one is mistreated or neglected, they might have very different IQs.

Unit 3:   Quest for Justice

Brown *vs.* Board of Education
by Walter Dean Myers

Study Skills: Using a Graphic Organizer (p. 15)

Suggested responses:

>step 2: summary
>
>step 3: review case
>
>step 4: briefs
>
>step 5: justices read
>
>step 6: lawyers argue
>
>step 7: justices discuss case

"A Retrieved Reformation"
by O. Henry

Cross-Curricular Connection: Science (p. 16)

Suggested responses:

A. 1. fingerprints and other evidence studied in laboratories such as fibers, blood, and hair, and DNA identification

2. He probably did not wear gloves because he would not have been concerned with leaving fingerprints.

3. telephone, television, and computer information to aid in the sharing of information, especially between police agencies

B. It would be more difficult for Jimmy to be a successful safe cracker today because of stronger bank vaults, electronic security, and modern police forensic science labs.

"Emancipation" from *Lincoln: A Photobiography* by Russell Freedman
"O Captain! My Captain!"
by Walt Whitman

Workplace Skills: Decision Making (p. 17)

Suggested responses:

A. 1. He wanted to defeat the rebellion, restore the Union, and abolish the institution of slavery.

2. The freed slaves would enlist in the Union army and participate in the defeat of the rebel forces. They would no longer be providing labor for the South's war effort. The quicker the defeat of the south, the quicker the unification of the country.

3. He could have allowed slavery to continue. He could have continued the war effort without the help of the freed slaves.

4. The war might not have settled the slavery issue. If the North lost the war, the institution of slavery would continue.

B. 1. Reason for decision: find an after-school job at local fast-food restaurant

2. Objectives: earn spending money; gain experience in the work world

3. Alternatives: baby-sit in the evenings

4. Consequences of alternatives: evening baby-sitting will cut into my social life; baby-sitting is not really considered workplace experience

5. Final course of action: apply for the fast-food job

"Gentleman of Rio en Medio"
by Juan A. A. Sedillo
"Saving the Wetlands"
by Barbara A. Lewis

Cross-Curricular Connection: Math (p. 18)

1. 16
2. 872 feet (217.8 × 4 = 871.2)
3. 800 feet (200 × 4 = 800)
4. 43,560 square feet (217.8 × 200 = 43,560)
5. $150.00 per acre (1,200 ÷ 8 = 150)
6. $2,400 (1,200 × 2 = 2,400)

"Raymond's Run"
by Toni Cade Bambara

Career Connection: Athletic Coach (p. 19)

Suggested responses:

A. 1. Students should mention demonstrating and explaining skills, teaching fundamentals of a sport, teaching safety, organizing and running a school sports program, and encouraging athletes to perform well.

2. Students should mention professional sports, college, high school, and middle school team sports programs, and individual instruction in various sports.

3. Students may mention patience, fairness, an easy-going nature, compassion, and a sense of humor.

B. Students may ask about the applicant's educational background and teaching experience, ability to manage and motivate students, and the ways in which the applicant might handle certain hypothetical situations.

"Paul Revere's Ride"
by Henry Wadsworth Longfellow

Cultural Connection: Heroes (p. 20)

Suggested responses:

A. 1. courage, wisdom, honesty, resourcefulness, perseverance

2. Students may mention the more male dominated society of the past.

3. Students may mention that heroes are often acknowledged more for their actions, than for other accomplishments.

4. Students may say that heroes are great role models; other students may say that heroes make unrealistic role models.

5. Students may say that our idea of a hero will remain the same because our basic nature will remain the same. Other students may say that our idea of a hero will be formulated by the expectations and demands of our culture in 100 years.

B. Students should support their ideas with specific examples and details.

"Always to Remember: The Vision of Maya Ying Lin"
by Brent Ashabranner

Humanities Connection: Fine Arts (p. 21)

Suggested responses:

A. 1. The Southern Poverty Law Center

2. "until justice rolls down like waters and righteousness like a mighty stream"

B. 1. Students may think of national or local individuals or causes. They should support their selections with reasoned arguments.

2. Students should consider the size or shape of the memorial and the effect it will have on visitors.

3. Students should support their answers with details about the importance of their memorial and the reasons people might visit it.

Unit 4:   From Sea to Shining Sea

from "The People, Yes"
by Carl Sandburg

Career Connection: How Jobs Change (p. 22)

Suggested responses:

A. 2. line 4, farmer, plants and sows crops

  3. line 10, beekeeper, raises bees and sells the honey

  4. line 11, railroad engineer, operates a train

  5. line 11, railroad conductor, collects tickets from passengers

  6. line 15, ship's captain, person in charge of a ship

  7. line 16, sailor, helps in the operation of a ship

  8. line 17, sheep farmer, raises sheep for wool and/or meat

B. farming

1. Students may say that the poem implies that farming is a difficult job because the farmer is not able to control the way in which the crop develops nor the effect of the weather on the crop.

2. Students may point out that the average size of a farm in the United States has more than doubled since the poem was written—from about 195 acres to about 440 acres. At the same time, the average cost of running a farm has increased nearly twenty times. Small family farms are increasingly giving way to larger farms owned by or rented to business partnerships or corporations. Today's farmers have access to computer programs to help them plan planting and harvesting and to make the most effective use of their land. Modern-day tractors, combines, and other machines make the grueling work easier than it once was. Temperature-controlled cabs, headlights, and other features enable the farmer to easily operate machinery in any weather and at any time of day. Farming remains a risky business, though, because the weather is still impossible to control.

from Travels with Charley
by John Steinbeck

Career Connection: Travel Writer (p. 23)

Suggested responses:

City: London, England

1. Drive from home in rural western New York to the airport in Rochester, New York. Fly to New York City, change plans for international flight to London, England; stay one week; two nights in a bed-and-breakfast and five nights in a hotel; plan to visit the Tower of London, a live theater production at Piccadilly Circus, and the British Museum.

2. Arrange in advance to interview the leading actor in the play, the director of the British Museum, and the head chef of the most popular restaurant in London.

3. city-specific travel guides, city and food-specific web sites, culinary magazines, city guide, materials from the chamber of commerce, local phone books

4. tape recorder for interviewing, tapes, batteries, camera and film, laptop computer, notepads, dictaphone, maps, list of contacts and phone numbers, plane tickets, prepared list of questions to ask during interviews.

"Choice: A Tribute to Dr. Martin Luther King, Jr." by Alice Walker
"The New Colossus"
by Emma Lazarus
"Ellis Island" by Joseph Bruchac
"Achieving the American Dream"
by Mario Cuomo

Cross-Curriculum Connection: Math (p. 24)

A. 1. 62 years (1954 minus 1892 = 62)

  2. 375,000 per year (12,000,000 divided by 32 = 375,000)

  3. $45,000 ($30.00 multiplied by 1,500 = $45,000.00)

B. 1. 1,820,906 (1,893,542 minus 72,636)

2. 6,032,684 (add all eight figures together)

3. 1,206,536.8 (6,032,684 divided by 5)

4. Germany with 633,148 immigrants

"A Ribbon for Baldy" by Jesse Stuart
"The White Umbrella" by Gish Jen

Cross-Curricular Connection: Science (p. 25)

Suggested responses:

1. low
2. cumulonimbus
3. fair weather cumulus
4. nimbostratus
5. cirrus
6. cirrus
7. fair weather cumulus
8. nimbostratus and cumulonimbus

"Those Winter Sundays"
by Robert Hayden
"Taught Me Purple"
by Evelyn Tooley Hunt
"The City Is So Big"
by Richard García

Cultural Connection: The Work Week (p. 26)

A. 1. doctor, airline pilot, newspaper reporter

2. restaurants, pharmacies

3. teacher, banker

4. plumber, doctor

B. Students may say that by extending the work week people can shop and conduct business whenever it suits them and do not have to program those tasks into specified hours between Monday and Friday. Students may say that a 7-day, 24-hour world makes it difficult to find rest and relaxation.

Unit 5:   Extraordinary Occurrences

"Lights in the Night"
from *An American Childhood*
by Annie Dillard

Cultural Connection: Shadow Puppets (p. 27)

1. The shows help tell the most important stories of the culture to each generation. Additionally, the shows are very entertaining.

2. The audience's imagination responds much more readily to night shadows than to those in bright sunlight.

3. *Wayang* means "shadow", and Indonesians have a saying that drama is the shadow of life.

4. The *dalang* is the shadow puppeteer who controls the puppets, does all the voice dialog, and sings songs during the long performance.

5. Students' answers should reflect the understanding that shadow puppetry can be used to tell stories of serious epic proportion or of more simple design.

"What Stumped the Blue Jays"
by Mark Twain
"Why Leaves Turn Color in the Fall"
by Diane Ackerman

Community Connection: Community Action (p. 28)

Suggested responses:

1. To involve people in a friendly project to aid home gardeners in recycling leaves into compost

2. Design and distribute fliers to announce project

3. Produce and distribute written directions on building a home compost bin

4. Build a demonstration compost bin and show how compost is made

5. Collect leaves for demonstration bin

6. County extension horticultural agent

7. Experienced home gardener

8. Friends and fellow club members

9. Pamphlets and directions written and printed

"What Stumped the Blue Jays"
by Mark Twain
"Why Leaves Turn Color in the Fall"
by Diane Ackerman
(continued)

10. Demonstration bins finished
11. People working together, pride in self suf-
ficiency, great use of a free resource,
healthy home gardens.

"The Story-Teller"
by Mark Van Doren
"Los New Yorks"
by Victor Hernández Cruz
"Southbound on the Freeway"
by May Swenson

Cross-Curricular Connection: Math (p. 29)

A. 1. 77,400; 143,549,627
   2. 7,673,145
   3. 81,261,766
   4. from 1990 to 1994
B. 1. 490,132,244
   2. the 1980s; increase of 171,869,252
   3. Students should support their answers
with reasons such as resource depletion,
overpopulation, new drivers in China,
smaller and cheaper cars.
   4. Students should support their answers
with reasonable conclusions.

"The Adventure of the Speckled Band" by Sir Arthur Conan Doyle

Career Connection: Detective (p. 30)
Suggested responses:

A. 1. He first used his skills for logical reasoning when he claimed that Helen Stoner
traveled by train to London.

2. He conducted a lengthy interview with
useful questions.
3. He first examined the window shutters
to Helen's room.
4. He made a thorough visual examination
of the entire room looking for information.

B. Suggested responses:
1. Honesty, intelligence, knowledge of people
2. Science to understand modern police techniques and psychology to understand people

"A Glow in the Dark" by Gary Paulsen
"Mushrooms" by Sylvia Plath
"Southern Mansion"
by Arna Bontemps
"The Bat" by Theodore Roethke

Cross-Curricular Connection: Science (p. 31)

1. The ability of a living organism to create
light.
2. It is the brightest light of any living organism; the light is created by bacteria on the
fish.
3. No sunlight reaches the deep ocean and
animals have evolved the ability to create
their own light.
4. Each species of firefly creates its own unique
patterns of light flashes to communicate.
5. Mushrooms or fungi growing on the wood
6. Students should provide reasonable answers about the experience.

Unit 6:   Short Stories

"The Tell-Tale Heart"
by Edgar Allan Poe

Career Connection: Set Designer (p. 32)
Suggested responses:

A. Setting: A two-story wooden farm-style
house. This house sits back from an iso-
lated, dirt road overgrown with weeds. It is
a house that is abandoned. Windows are
shattered; tangled vines grow around the
chimney. The vines hide the front porch.
The front door hangs off of its hinges. The
wood siding is faded. At the back of the
house is a barn that is new by comparison.

Props: Props can include things to dress the scene or things someone in the film will use, such as a rope. Anything can be listed here from rugs to coffee mugs to an ax.

Lighting: Students should consider the time of day and the best lighting to set the mood.

B. Students should describe specifically the setting, props, and lighting.

"Hamadi" by Naomi Shihab Nye
"The Day I Got Lost"
by Isaac Bashevis Singer

Study Skills: Map Reading (p. 33)

A. 1. south

2. southeast

3. west

4. south, west

5. northwest

6. northeast

7. north, east

8. east, north

"The Finish of Patsy Barnes"
by Paul Laurence Dunbar
"Tears of Autumn"
by Yoshiko Uchida

Study Skills: Making an Outline (p. 34)

Suggested responses:

A. 1. Mother, Taro Takedo

2. Mother talks with others, Taro plans Hana's trip to America

3. Mother: talks with Hana's sisters and their husbands, talks with village priest

Taro: sends money for steamship passage, arranges for Hana to stay with friends upon arrival

B. Outline:

I. Mother

  A. Talks with others

    1. talks to sisters and husbands

    2. talks to village priest

II. Taro Takedo

  A. Plans for Hana's trip to America

    1. sends money for steamship passage

    2. arranges for Hana to stay with friends upon arrival

"The Medicine Bag"
by Virginia Driving Hawk Sneve
"The Story-Teller" by Saki

Community Connection: Parks (p. 35)

Suggested responses:

A. Neighborhood: Landscape—planted gardens, bicycle paths; Natural Inhabitants—pigeons, rabbits; Activities—swimming, picnics; Facilities—wading pool, picnic tables

Wilderness: Landscape—mountains, river, forests; Natural Inhabitants—prairie dogs, bear, snakes; Activities—backpacking, fishing, hunting; Facilities—campground, hiking trail signs, hunting cabins

Historic: Landscape—monuments, dedicated paths with historic markers, historic homes; Natural Inhabitants—people, birds, mice; Activities—ranger-led programs, reenactments, brief films; Facilities—visitor center, bookstore, museum

B. A community park could be one with a bandstand and a wading pool with water fountain. It could have landscaped walking and bike paths, outdoor grill areas, or a small petting zoo. Activities would include picnicking, ball games, volleyball, swimming or rollerblading. It is a park where events help families celebrate the major holidays, such as the Fourth of July, Memorial Day, and Labor Day. These events include fireworks, band concerts, carnivals, and games. It is a place in which families and friends gather. All generations come together here.

"Animal Craftsmen" by Bruce Brooks

Cross-Curricular Connection: Science (p. 36)

A. Suggested responses:

1. Students should indicate if the animal requires a warm or cool climate, or if the animal can live comfortably in any climate.

2. Students should indicate in which geographic locale it is found, such as the mountains, grasslands, tropical forests, desert, polar region, ocean, etc.

3. Students might list natural materials (such as wood, straw, and twigs) or materials produced by the animal's own body (such as a spider's thread for a web).

4. Students should mention particular vegetation, fish or other animals.

5. Students might mention any requirements not covered previously under the categories of food, shelter, and location.

6. Students might mention things such as treating animals gently, not hunting them, and not destroying their homes.

B. Suggested responses: Students may add captions and marginal notes to their drawings to indicate how their designs facilitate and benefit the animals.

from *One Writer's Beginnings*
by Eudora Welty
"Baseball" by Lionel G. García

Study Skills: Outlining (p. 37)

Suggested responses:

I. The name of the game might indicate something about the equipment needed to play or the way the game is played.

II. Equipment or materials might include balls, nets, boards, dice, or spinners, for example.

III. The goal might be to score the most or fewest points, or to outlast an opponent in another way.

IV. Make sure students present their steps in a chronological order that makes the game easy to understand.

V. Students should mention special rules that are not covered in the procedures listed in part IV of the outline.

"Hokusai: The Old Man Mad About Drawing" by Stephen Longstreet
"Not to Go With the Others"
by John Hersey

Media Connection: Film Documentary (p. 38)

Suggested responses:

1. Students might mention traits such as leadership, strength, friendliness, intelligence, or a sense of humor. Students should make clear why they have selected each event and how it reflects upon their character.

2. Students may choose incidents of which they are personally aware or may choose events and stories told to them by others.

3. Students should choose to interview the subject's family members, friends, or neighbors who have intimate knowledge of the subject's life and personality.

4. Students who do not choose chronological order might choose a sequence involving flashbacks, or perhaps an order based on stories and events told by the subject's friends and family.

"Debbie" by James Herriot
"Forest Fire" by Anais Nïn

Workplace Skills: Acting Responsibly (p. 39)

Suggested responses:

1. Students might say they would look for the book in another library or in a bookstore in order to have a copy for an extended period of time.

2. Students might say that it is more important to tell the truth, because a lie might get their friends in deeper trouble later on.

3. Students might say they would leave a small tip.

4. Students might say that they would not call their friends but would seek an extension in handing in the assignment.

"The Trouble with Television"
by Robert MacNeil
"The American Dream"
by Martin Luther King, Jr.

Cultural Connection: Television and Society (p. 40)

A. Suggested responses:

1. Students may say that television news and documentaries tend to focus primarily on the problems of teens rather than on their accomplishments. Students may say that many dramas and situation comedies portray teenagers in more typical settings.

2. Students may say that news and information programs are fairly accurate in their depiction of problems in schools but that such programs tend to cover a narrow range of schools. Some students may say that the portrayal of schools in fictional accounts on television is fairly well balanced.

3. Students may have widely different views on how family life is portrayed on television. Students should support their answers with examples.

B. Students should describe the tone of the show (humorous or serious, for example) as well as its format, such as a sitcom, talk show, news broadcast, or other venue.

Unit 8:   Drama

The Diary of Anne Frank, Act I
by Frances Goodrich and Albert Hackett

Cross-Curricular Connection: Art (p. 41)

Suggested responses:

1. Students may say that Anne Frank's courage was most impressive.

2. Students may say that they would like people to know that Anne Frank was in some ways a typical teenager who was forced to live in extraordinary times.

3. Students may say that they would like people to remember Anne Frank for her humor and ability to make the best of the worst possible situation.

4. Students may want to express these ideas symbolically or realistically. For example, they might create a figure looking up at the sky with arm outstretched smiling as she releases a bird.

5. Students may create a message of their own or use a famous quotation from Anne's diary or from another source.

The Diary of Anne Frank, Act II
by Frances Goodrich and Albert Hackett

Humanities Connection: Philosophy (p.42)

Suggested responses:

1. Some students may maintain that breaking the law is never justified. Others might argue that it's allowed in order to save a life.

2. Students might say that children past a certain age should not be treated as if they were incapable of acting maturely or of being trusted.

3. Students should explain why they have chosen that particular age as the starting point for serious social relationships.

4. Some students may argue that self-preservation is of utmost importance. Others may maintain that sharing, even at the risk of losing your own life, is essential.

5. Students might argue that if a choice must be made between saving a human or an animal, a human life takes precedence.

6. Some students may argue that young people deserve more because they haven't yet experienced that which adults already have.

7. Some students may maintain that all people are basically good if they are treated fairly.

Unit 9:   Poetry

"The Secret Heart"
by Robert P. Tristram Coffin

Cross-Curricular Connection: Science (p. 43)

1. to the upper right chamber, the right atrium
2. carbon dioxide
3. pumps blood to the lungs
4. to the upper left chamber of the heart, the left atrium
5. It is pumped from the lower left chamber of the heart, the left ventricle.

"The Wreck of the Hesperus"
by Henry Wadsworth Longfellow
"The Centaur" by May Swenson

Study Skills: Reading Graphic Organizers (p. 44)

Students should describe the increasing size of waves and crests. They should mention the increasing number of whitecaps and the increasing amounts of spray and foam. They should mention that visibility became increasingly bad.

"Harlem Night Song" by Langston Hughes
"Blow, Blow, Thou Winter Wind" by William Shakespeare
"love is a place" by E. E. Cummings
"January" by John Updike

Career Connection: Meteorologist (p. 45)

1. They predict the weather.
2. They work in weather research.
3. They develop new tools for forecasting the weather.
4. They collect and analyze past records of the weather in specific areas.
5. a bachelor's degree with courses in meteorology, advanced math, physics, statistics, and computer science, among other things

"Ode to Enchanted Light"
by Pablo Neruda
Two Haiku by Bashō and Moritake
"She Dwelt Among the Untrodden Ways" by William Wordsworth
"Harriet Beecher Stowe"
by Paul Laurence Dunbar
from "John Brown's Body"
by Stephen Vincent Benét
"400-Meter Free Style"
by Maxine Kumin

Cross-Curricular Connection: Science (p. 46)

Stage 1: Eggs—the eggs are laid on the kind of food that the caterpillar, the next stage, will eat. Stage 2: Caterpillar—the main job of the caterpillar is to eat and store food for the chrysalis, the next stage. Stage 3: Chrysalis—the butterfly forms inside this protective covering. Stage 4: Butterfly—this is the adult stage. The main job of the adult butterfly is to mate and let the process begin again.

"Silver" by Walter de la Mare
"Forgotten Language"
by Shel Silverstein
"Drum Song" by Wendy Rose
"If I can stop one Heart from breaking" by Emily Dickinson

Study Skills: Using a Graphic Organizer (p. 47)

dog: fur, four, none
dove: feathers, two, two
mouse: fur, four, none
fish: scales, none, none
caterpillar: skin, six, none
starling: feathers, two, two
housefly: fine hair, six, two
cricket: fine hair, six, two pairs
turtle: shell, four, none
woodpecker: feathers, two, two
snow hare: fur, four, none
owl: feathers, two, two
robin: feathers, two, two

In column 5, students might use such headings as "Good pet?," "Kind of noise it makes," "What it eats," "Where it lives," or "Enemies."

"New World" by N. Scott Momaday
"Lyric 17" by José Garcia Villa
"For My Sister Molly Who in the Fifties" by Alice Walker

Cultural Connection: The Pulitzer Prize (p. 48)

1. He became the owner and publisher of two newspapers, the *St. Louis Post-Dispatch* and the *New York World.*
2. partial blindness
3. Columbia University
4. the Pulitzer Prize Board
5. American journalism, letters (fiction, history, poetry, biography or autobiography, and general nonfiction), drama, and music
6. No. The awards are given for achievements only in American journalism, letters, drama, and music.

"The Dark Hills"
by Edwin Arlington Robinson
"Incident in a Rose Garden"
by Donald Justice

Study Skills: Using an Outline (p. 49)

Student's outlines should resemble the following.

A. Watering
  1. Basin flooding
  2. Drip irrigation
  3. Overhead sprinkling
    a. Advantages
      i. Removes dust
      ii. Freshens the foliage
    b. Disadvantage: Encourages foliage diseases with the dampness
B. Nutrients
  1. Dry commercial fertilizers, added to the soil
  2. Liquid fertilizers, added to water or sprayed on rose leaves
C. Pest and disease control
  1. Aphids, spider mites, and thrips
    a. mechanical controls
      i. hand-picking
      ii. strong jet of water
    b. control by other insects
    c. soaps and special oils
  2. Mildew, rust, and black spot—chemical controls

Unit 10:   The American Folk Tradition

"Chicoria" by José Griego y Maestas and Rudolfo A. Anaya
"Brer Possum's Dilemma" by Jackie Torrence
"Why the Waves Have Whitecaps" by Zora Neale Hurston
"Coyote Steals the Sun and Moon," retold by Richard Erdoes and Alfonso Ortiz

Cross-Curricular Connection: Science (p. 50)

1. crest
2. trough
3. wavelength
4. height
5. Waves would also go in different directions.
6. It would bob up and down.
7. It would go up and down with the waves, unless the waves got so big that they broke over the boat, breaking and sinking it.

"John Henry" Traditional
"Paul Bunyan of the North Woods"
by Carl Sandburg
"Pecos Bill: The Cyclone"
by Harold W. Felton
"Davy Crockett's Dream"
by Davy Crockett

Workplace Skills: Goal Setting (p. 51)

Guidelines for student responses:

A. Students should mention the following goals: John Henry wanted to be a steel-driving man and achieved success through hard work and determination. Paul Bunyan had many goals, including one of stopping the rain on the Fourth of July; he achieved this goal by climbing up a pillar of water that was coming down and turning it off. Pecos Bill's goals included fencing Texas and parts of Arizona and New Mexico. He achieved this goal by getting prairie dogs to dig the holes, and then he put a post in each hole. He also tamed a cyclone on the Fourth of July because it was threatening to ruin the celebration. Davy Crockett's goals included getting some dinner for himself and his wife; to accomplish this goal, he went out hunting in the snow. Even though he didn't accomplish the goal, he did his best to achieve it.

B. Students' goals might include getting good grades, learning to play a musical instrument, being part of a sports team, learning more about computers, becoming more skilled at skate-boarding, learning a foreign language, and so on.